CW00762284

THE STARS ✳
✳ OVER PAXOS

THE STARS ✳
✳ OVER PAXOS

JOHN GILL

PAVILION

First published in Great Britain in 1995 by
Pavilion Books Limited
26 Upper Ground
London SE1 9PD

Text copyright © by John Gill
The moral right of the author has been asserted

Cover illustration and black and white decorations
copyright © by Madeleine David

Designed by Nigel Partridge

All rights reserved. No part of this publication may be
reproduced, stored in a retrieval system, or transmitted in any
form or by any means, electronic, mechanical, photocopying,
recording, or otherwise, without the prior permission of the
copyright owner.

A CIP catalogue record for this book is available from the
British Library

ISBN 1-85793-351 6

Printed and bound in Great Britain by Butler & Tanner Limited

2 4 6 8 10 9 7 5 3 1

This book may be ordered by post direct from the publisher.
Please contact the Marketing Department.
But try your bookshop first.

CONTENTS

Για τον Ντον, φυσικά,
και τους φίλους του, ιδιαιτέρως για τον
Παναγιώτη Βασσιλά και την οικογένεια του.

For Don, of course, and his friends,
especially Panayiotis Vassilas and his family

HEAVEN

I HAVE DISCOVERED my idea of heaven on Earth. It is an end-less game of Scrabble on this clifftop terrace, lit by a Paxos sunset in which the sun never ever sets. Our gin and tonics are eternally iced and always full, and we never run out of peanuts. Miles Davis's *Kind of Blue* plays in the background, and it goes on forever . . .

ONE

 KRONIA POLLA

CHRISTMAS DAY ON PAXOS, and two women are picking olives in the olive groves that surround a friend's house in the south of the island while I prepare a Christmas meal in her kitchen. This is now the third year in succession that the normally biennial olive crop has bloomed, giving a meagre crop amounting in places to barely a third or even a quarter of its normal yield. In normal olive years, most growers wouldn't even be harvesting their olives yet, but ferocious November storms brought down much of the crop, forcing islanders out into the olive groves to pick the olives from the nets laid beneath the trees before the olives began to rot. When the harvest is so poor, nothing can be allowed to go to waste. The work in the olive groves is the last link with this island's peasant history. While Paxos strains to

8

move on into a post-industrial leisure economy built on tourism, services and property, something it might find easier to do than Britain, the olive groves yoke it still to its agrarian past.

This small green island, barely seven miles by three, ten miles south of the southernmost tip of Corfu and ten miles west of the Greek mainland, has relied on its olive crop since the trees were first introduced over 500 years ago by Venetian invaders. Its olive harvest has been the backbone of its economy, its sole source of wealth, for centuries, and the daily lives of the islanders have been dominated by the olive crop since the times of Geoffrey Chaucer.

Which is why the women were frequently outdoors on this feast day, heaping the fallen olives into the centre of the black plastic nets, picking out the larger leaves, sticks and other debris, scooping the olives into a wooden box with a slatted bottom that would allow finer debris to fall out when shaken, winnowing and picking again, and dumping the sorted olives into sacks. I spent much of the day in my friend's kitchen, improvising an English Christmas meal – imported turkey, local potatoes roasted in Paxos olive oil, sprouts from Epirus on the mainland, apple and nut stuffing from local fruit and herbs, bread sauce, and Greek wines, English gin and Finnish vodka for toasts to absent friends – and whenever I looked out of the big kitchen window they were out there again, gleaning single olives from the paths that run through the groves, even picking them from where they had fallen into bushes and shrubs. By the end of the afternoon, when twilight began to fall, I doubt that they had managed to fill just one sack. At one point a man came to join them, staying to watch for a short while, then leaving. Pat, the friend I was cooking for, said this was typical, both of her neighbour and of Greek men in general.

9

We followed our Christmas meal with the finest that Greek television could offer: a choice of *Gone with the Wind*, the Greek version of *Blind Date*, which is even tack-ier than its English counterpart, or variety programmes that seemed to be styled in the manner of British light entertainment from the 1950s. I somehow doubted, however, that Pat's neighbours spent their evening slumped sated in front of a colour television making snide comments about Clark Gable's finest hour. They were out in the olive groves until after darkness began to creep through the trees, and then disappeared into a barely lit traditional Greek cottage.

Gone with the Wind was crap anyway, even if they had been able to watch it: by the time Rhett told Scarlett that, frankly, he didn't give-a-damn (and Clark Gable actually pronounces the hyphens there) we were expressing similar misgivings about the film itself. We cheered the burning of Atlanta and the destruction of Tara, and went to bed.

While the Greek Orthodox Easter is the biggest Hellenic celebration of the year, a mixture of New Year and Christmas Day with some Christian death-and-resurrection ritual thrown in for good measure, Paxiots and mainlanders alike do celebrate Christmas. They exchange presents, cook turkey, although more likely as a stew than as a roast, throw parties, and decorate Christmas trees improvised from the abundant varieties of evergreens and baby pines on the island. One friend even has a 'pet' tree in the hills above the village which she uproots each year, decorates in her home, and then replants in the same spot after twelfth night.

As Christmas approaches, trees appear in the squares of the island's three harbour villages: Gaios, its capital, Lakka, my spiritual home on this island paradise, and tiny Loggos.

Rumour even has it that local wags sneak out at night in Lakka and decorate the tree with inflated condoms, although I never saw the condoms appear at all the Christmas I was in Lakka. In Gaios's one small square, the tree is kept company by a large crib, and one which goes unmolested, just like the trees, throughout the Christmas season. In a curious collision of cultures, islanders also employ both English and Greek greetings, freely swapping between Merry Christmas, Happy New Year and the generic Greek greeting, *Kronia Polla*, loosely, 'many years', which is used at Christmas, Easter and on individual Name Days, the saints' days that take the place of birthday celebrations in Greece. Perhaps most unusual of all, however, is the Greek passion for Christmas decoration. People erect lavish miniature versions of the Regent Street illuminations in their homes and villages, and take the Father Christmas/snow theme to bizarre extremes. Strolling around Gaios's elegant Venetian harbour front one warm and sunny day just before Christmas, garbed only in jeans, T-shirt and sneakers in this balmy weather and wishing I'd remembered to bring some sunglasses, I was taken aback by stencilled 'KRONIA POLLA' signs in people's windows, decorated with large frosted snowflakes, and here, on an island where it has snowed perhaps once in the last quarter-century (news that the Paxiot diaspora carried halfway round the world), some people had gone to the bother of actually spraying tiny snowdrifts in the corners of each windowpane. Even here, on an island where parts of the terrain resemble biblical desert, the mythology of Father Christmas and the frozen north has gained a tenacious hold. Wealthier islanders even take their children to Corfu to see Father Christmas in his snowy grotto in a department store. This, in weather that is more summery than some Mays I've spent on the island.

This phenomenon is not special to the Ionian, or indeed Greece as a whole: American sunbelt cities like Atlanta and New Orleans sprout Christmas finery, as indeed do subtropical Mexican cities like Oaxaca and Merida, but these are places rooted in either the WASP Christmas tradition or Roman Catholicism. Having been in these places around Christmas time, I can remember the strange sense of dislocation at encountering Christmas traditions in such hot climes, but in a place where WASP culture is alien, something impermanent that normally arrives and departs on ferries during the summer, the sense of dislocation, and even a certain sense of cultural invasion, becomes acute.

Christmas is an altogether strange, and actually quite beautiful, time on Paxos, and for reasons other than the foregoing. Winter on this small green island has its own mythology among summer visitors, something to which I subscribed during the last decade or so of visiting Paxos. Everyone who visits the island soon learns about the water shortages, the lack of artesian water supplies which for centuries has meant that the population have to trap rainwater from their roofs and pipe it into room-sized tanks, or *sternas*, for use during the summer. Dry winters can mean summers where there is not enough water to go around, where tourists may even be evacuated from Loggos, as I once witnessed, because water was running out at the end of the season. Baths, in the few properties that have them, are frowned on by travel companies, tour operators and local accommodation agencies. Notes in most tourist properties beg visitors to be sparing in their use of water. Few houses or commercial properties expect guests to flush the toilet if they are only taking a piss, and at the friend's house in the hills above Lakka where I stay, men are expected to take a leak at the end of the (thankfully rather leafy) garden. If it's raining or the middle of the night, and outmoded decorum permits, you just piss out the door.

There is now a fairly extensive system that pipes *glypha*, desalinated sea water, to most houses on the island, and in parts this will soon be replaced by new reservoirs pumping freshly filtered rainwater through the *glypha* pipes. But the sweet *sterna* rainwater, cleaner than anything coming out of London taps, is still jealously guarded, often literally; many *sternas* have padlocks on them, and at least one I have seen is actually surrounded by barbed wire. Drought looms large in the history of Paxos, and there are old people on the island who remember droughts so bad that islanders were reduced to drinking olive oil to slake their thirst.

The winter rains that replenish the *sternas* and the reservoirs are a major factor in the mythology of the Paxos winter. Anyone who has dallied on the island into October and November will have been through at least one Paxos storm: lashing hurricane-force gales that can last days and days and days, inundating the square in Gaios and flooding Lakka with as much as a foot of rainwater that is unable to flow into the sea fast enough to clear the village. The nearest equivalent to stepping outside in one of these things would probably be walking fully dressed through the rinse stage of a carwash.

The Paxos winter, then, is a thing of legend, crashing storms and housebound locals sent mad by cabin fever. Everything's shut – bars, restaurants, shops – and those few shops that remain open have very little to sell, anyway. The islanders probably revert to the pre-nineteenth-century practice of netting birds on the cliffs to eat, and other traditions best left undescribed. In short, Paxos in winter was a water-themed new level from Dante's Inferno.

Returning to the island for my first Christmas, I packed

· 13

accordingly. Only William Boot, the hapless hero of Evelyn Waugh's *Scoop*, went more prepared. Foul weather clothing. Jumpers. Thick underwear. Foodstuffs that took up half the baggage space. A library of books. Waterproofs that might have enabled me to go deep-sea diving. A barometer, rain gauge, max-min thermometer, a device for calculating likely weather trends from this information, in fact everything but the Stevenson screen itself. Binoculars, computer, several books on astronomy, BBC Greek language course and the *Oxford Dictionary of Modern Greek*. Six pounds of plain brown flour and the yeast to make my own bread. There was also a silver rain cape that made me look like the monster from a 1950s science fiction movie and caused friends to laugh so hard they got the bends. One or two cleft sticks would have completed the ensemble.

It was a pleasant 65 degrees Fahrenheit when, thus encumbered, I arrived back at Corfu airport a fortnight before Christmas. More, the crowds who make Corfu town, and its airport, such a nightmare in the summer, were nowhere to be seen. I was through customs and baggage and into a taxi in less than fifteen minutes – *Jim'll Fix It* timing compared to the summer – and booked into a hotel in the town's Old Port in under thirty. The following day I took a ferry to Paxos, the high-speed *Pegasus* that cuts the customary three-hour slog in half. The Steno Paxon strait between the southern tip of Corfu and the northern tip of Paxos, a white-knuckle ride on some summer crossings, was so calm you could watch the reflection of the clouds sailing overhead. I stood in the open at the stern of the ninety-seater speedboat as we crossed, wondering if the sun low in the west was strong enough to start a suntan. It felt that warm.

The island's buses, which ply its one main road three times a day in season or during school term-time, never run on Sundays, a fact that has caught out many a tourist leaving on a Monday transfer and hoping for one last look at another part of the island on the Sunday. I arrived on a Saturday, staying with Pat at her house in Makratika, outside the capital Gaios, and decided to walk to Lakka in the north the following day.

Sunlight bathed the olive groves around Pat's house that Sunday morning. After ten minutes on the road to Lakka, the waterproof storm coat I'd bought for the trip came off, its lining damp with sweat from the heat. Soon I was down to jeans and T-shirt, virtually dragging the bad weather clothing behind me. Reaching the orange and red campanile of Haralambos church just beyond Bogdanatika, a mile or so further on, I dropped everything at the side of the road and sat down for a breather. At this elevation at the centre of the island, the towering cliffs of the west coast were below me, and beyond the sea glinted in the sunshine. The sun was so hot even the light breeze felt warm on the skin, conditions I remembered from summers on the island but hadn't associated with its winters.

Occasionally, islanders whizzed by in their cars, bemused at this bagperson basking by the side of the road and perhaps mistaking me for another of the Albanian refugees who are trying to build new lives on the island. One or two islanders who knew me stopped and offered lifts, and were bemused when I smiled and refused, explaining that I was on foot and actually wanted to walk. This would not be the first time they'd encountered a mad tourist, nor would it be the last.

I reached the village in perhaps an hour and a half, catching tantalising glimpses of the Ionian on both sides at almost every turn. Even on previous walks along the road that follows the island's spine, I had not noticed that the sea was so visible, sometimes simultaneously on either side, from the road. The bus that whiplashes around the island's hairpin bends affords only the occasional hurtling glimpse of these views, which on foot become a long succession of one stunning seascape after another.

Lakka, a collection of two or three tiny squares and a jumble of short alleys surrounded by low hills that protect a spectacular horseshoe bay, was deserted and virtually silent, save for the odd cock-crow or bark up in the hills. Apart from a few caiques and two yachts that winter there, the bay was empty of its usual clutter of summer traffic. The water was up high and glassy smooth, producing a disconcerting visual effect. It reminded me of an avant-garde sculpture installation in London, by the artist Richard Wilson, who filled a room of the Saatchi Gallery with oil and sank a walkway into it, so that the visitor walked into the centre of the oil, with the oil at waist-height, its meniscus trembling on the edge of the sunken walkway. Standing in the centre of Wilson's sculpture, the visitor experienced a sort of vertigo, and an incredible sense of latent danger. That Sunday at the edge of Lakka bay, as I lounged on the jetty drinking a beer in the sun and the extraordinary silence, the temporary owner of this air and water and rock, the surface of the water seemed far higher than it should have been, as though I was somehow immersed in it.

This first night, after opening up the little house hidden in the tree-covered hills above the village, I baked bread, which has become both therapy and religion for me, and sat in the garden watching the sun sink in the west. The house is tiny: two rooms barely 12 feet square each, a kitchen the size of a cupboard (but better equipped than any kitchen I've seen) a tiny loo and an outdoor cold-water shower. Its garden, however, has to have one of the most breathtaking private views in Greece; through the trees above the village, across the bay and out to sea with Corfu floating in the distance.

The winter crept back into the garden as the sun left it; a wind from the north, and a damp chill that seemed to rise from the ground. Incredibly, there were mosquitoes about. After a meal of emergency rations brought from Corfu – eggs, beans, bread, *retsina* – I buried myself beneath piled blankets to wait for sunrise.

Dawn brought another warm, cloudless day, the water in the bay as improbably clear and still as a turquoise jelly. The absence of the summer's noises, and the summer's people, gave Lakka an eerie, deserted atmosphere, as though it had been evacuated, or had been visited by some science-fiction disaster, like the closing reels of *On the Beach*. Odder still, however, was that it should be so deserted in such wonderful summery weather. I began to wonder if the mythology of the Paxiot winter really was precisely that, a myth to scare the summer visitors. My first encounter with a villager on this visit suggested that might not be far from the truth.

The mythology holds that, during the winter, the two village stores creak open only occasionally, and then you're lucky to find one can of spam on the shelves and a few vegetables that have been curling up on the racks outside since October. Both Steve's Yacht Stores, as the older of the two rather wishfully calls itself these days, and the Aronis family mini-market, whose marvellous legend, 'Shopping Here Is A Pleasure', produces knowing smirks in anyone who has shopped there, were open. Spiro Aronis, who runs the mini-market with his father, was behind his till, and in fact his shop looked remarkably well-stocked. Spiro is in his late thirties, educated, left-wing and speaks good English. If Lakka were ever to publish a list of its most eligible bachelors, Spiro would be quite near the top.

'So you caught us out,' he said, before I'd even uttered a word, before, in fact, I was inside his shop.

'What do you mean?'

'The weather,' he said; well, in fact, he said, 'the wezzah,' but as we could both make cheap phonetic cracks about each other's accents, and since Spiro had scolded me in the past for my lamentable attempts at Greek, I wasn't going to start correcting his English.

'Lovely weather,' he said. 'Have you been swimming yet?'

This could have been Spiro's own little joke – he knew that when I and my partner, Graham, visit in the summer, we rarely leave the garden, still less go swimming – or just another example of his surreal sense of humour. Perhaps bored by having to spend so much time behind his counter, Spiro sometimes deliberately scares strangers by making bizarrely cryptic comments to them and then laughing when they look baffled or embarrassed. One day, he asked me if I knew who I had been in a previous life. The next day, he asked me if I knew a vet. I asked if he was doing this on purpose. 'Yes!' he said, creasing with laughter. Still, this is preferable to his towering rages, although these, thankfully, are usually directed at Germans, Italians, and Greeks who don't vote for PASOK. Spiro's tempers have caused some unwary visitors to flee his store in terror. I once told him, 'You scare me when you're angry,' and he chuckled in a way that suggested I had just made his day.

I explained that, no, I hadn't been swimming yet, and was probably going to leave it a good five months or so until I did. Spiro simply chuckled, said 'No swimming, eh?' and began diddling with his pocket calculator. I could hear him still chuckling as I left his shop.

The strangest thing, however, was that all Spiro should do when I materialise in his village in the deepest midwinter, when even many expatriates have fled the island, is crack a joke. He was perfectly unfazed: no preamble, no look of surprise, no greeting and no questions about my sudden arrival in Lakka when I should really have been Christmas shopping in London. Spiro must have seen some surprising things in his time, and over the years I have become a fairly regular customer of his, but not even that could fully explain his breezy insouciance at my sudden arrival. It might have been September again, and I was just popping back because I'd forgotten the milk. Of course, it would be nice to think that I had become part of the furniture, but it's more likely that Spiro's lack of interest in the reasons for my arrival was the famous Greek cool that can greet the most bizarre notions with equanimity, a willingness to believe things, from superstition to science fiction, which verges on magic realism.

Others were less laid back. Nancy Grammatikos, a Chicagoan married to a Paxiot, Yiannis Grammatikos, did a doubletake when I rounded a corner, and, after the usual greetings, she seemed surprised that I had actually *chosen* to return to Paxos in midwinter. So did Sharon Grammatikos, who with her husband Tuli runs the Serano bar in the main square in the village, where the serious drinkers and summer party animals hang out till late (meaning, really, till early). Sharon is the one who has the pet Christmas tree up in the hills. Out of season, the Serano gets a regular trickle of customers in the evening, and earlier on teenagers congregate to bathe in the sickly green glow of two video-game machines at the back of the bar. This afternoon, however, Sharon and Tuli were pottering alone in their bar.

Apart from Nancy, Sharon and Tuli, the village was deserted. I wandered its alleyways and squares marvelling at the silence, the emptiness, the resonating absence. Even the islanders who live and work in the village during the summer had gone home for the winter. Lakka was hibernating. It has only one proper road going through it, although a few of the alleys are navigable by car, and when I first came to Lakka the one road used to be blocked off at night. But now nothing moved through its byways. Even the cats had quit the streets.

I returned to the house, for a lunch of bread, cheese and wine in the garden, marvelling even more at the idea of sitting eating lunch in the sun so near to Christmas. Again, winter rose with the mosquitoes when the sun sank in the west, framed between the two limestone cliffs of a col, or saddle, in the promontory on the western side of the horseshoe bay, shooting light up into the streaky altocumulus and producing a sunset like a Turner painting.

Shortly after six, I set off for the village, hoping to find friends who were anxious to hear news of a friend who was recovering from an operation in London. Apart from Serano, the only bar that would be open on a winter's evening was Spiro Petrou's kafeneon, a bar immortalised in the books of actor and writer Peter Bull thirty years ago. While numerous bars have since opened in Lakka to attract tourist business and flare briefly as the in place to drink and pose, Spiro's kafeneon has remained a constant in Lakka: a social centre for villagers, the most likely place to meet Greek friends, a place to find breakfast, ice cream after dinner, newspapers, telephones, free television and the rolling games of cards that seem to have been going on at some tables for years. It is also a little old-fashioned, a bit scruffy, and the last place on earth where the poseurs who plague Lakka in the summer would let themselves be seen. It is a safe haven in a mad world, a small theatre through which most village dramas will eventually pass, and its benign,

20

imperturbable owner, smiling behind his spectacles, brings light and kindness back into my world every time he greets me. (Spiro does, however, also suffer from the magic realism. The actress Susannah York has a house on Paxos, at this end of the island. One autumn, bidding Spiro farewell, I explained I was going back to my job in London. Presuming us to be neighbours in the way that Paxiots are neighbours, he asked me to send his regards to Susannah York.)

Negotiating the landscape of Paxos alone at night was something new in itself. The path out of the village up to the house, passing through scrub, bush and trees, is fairly dark at night. Anyone using it at night needs a torch, and a torch to themselves to watch where they are treading. I'd negotiated the path alone just once before, after a trip to the mainland when I'd returned early feeling ill, leaving Graham and our host, Don, to eat in the village. As some-one who checks each room of the house for maniacs every time I return home alone at night, I mounted the path out of the village certain that Freddie, Jason, Hannibal and the pasty-faced guy from *Halloween* were waiting, poised, behind each shadowy bush and tree I passed – well, ran by. Safely home, I locked myself in until it seemed likely that Freddie, Jason and Co would have gone in search of prey elsewhere. Until, in fact, it seemed likely that Graham and Don were due to return and wonder why on Earth they were locked out of the house.

The fact that Paxos out of season offered slim pickings for cruelly inventive serial killers didn't lessen the terror of the darkness, darkness made spookier by the fact that there were no businesses with their lights on in the village, but the win-ter stillness did make the irrational fear seem silly enough to render the journey harmless. In fact, Paxos in the winter darkness cured my fear of the dark – or at least, the dark on

Paxos. These became nights of wonder; spectacular sunsets, breathtaking cloudscapes lit by the moon, the inky silhouettes of the hills and treelines circling Lakka, starfields I had never seen before. In winter more than the summer, the stars over Paxos are magical, dazzling, and remind me of Marlowe's marvellous line for the doomed Faustus, 'See, where God's blood streams in the firmament!'

Lakka at night in winter was like no Lakka I had seen before, either. Neither Steve's nor the mini-market was open that Monday evening, and although Serano's was open in the square the only light I could find in the village was the homely yellow glow from Spiro Petrou's kafeneon. If I hadn't known it was there I could have just followed the noise: half the village seemed to have crammed themselves into the kafeneon. They were, of course, mostly men, but there were also women and children there too. Spiro's obviously became a refuge for the housebound on these winter evenings. The air was smoky and the babble of conversation loud, and there were few seats available. Before I had taken two steps into the room, I was surrounded by villagers wanting news of our friend in London; news, moreover, that my lazy Greek was unable to impart fully. My version of the Greek word for operation baffled them, and I had to make do with the fact that he was well and would be returning to the island soon. Their concern was touching, familial, and went far beyond mere neighbourliness, a concept most Londoners have learned to live without. It really did seem like the quality of philoxenia, the love of strangers, that is said to be gradually disappearing from other parts of Greece. There are monsters on this island, and in this village, capable of the most appalling behaviour, but they are rare exceptions among a people whose kindness and affection restore this cynic's faith in humanity.

I was looking for Panayiotis Vassilas, my sometime employer in the olive groves in Vasilatika, his family's tiny village high on the cliffs of the west coast. Pano is our greatest friend on Paxos, a man of unfailing kindness and grace, qualities matched only by his limitless capacity for laughter and mischief. Pano is barely five foot six, one of those incredibly slim Greeks who seem to have waists you could circle with index fingers and thumbs. He has a pianist's hands, large but dextrous, although this is a pianist with dirt under his fingernails. As well as an olive grower, he is also one of the island's small band of taxi-drivers (and immortalised, anonymously but unmistakably, in a Mills and Boon romance, Anne Weale's *Passage to Paxos*) and a builder. His family is one of the oldest on the island, and their village, Vasilatika, little more than a hamlet, really, has been a safe haven from bandits, pirates and other invaders since the Middle Ages. He, his wife Marianthi, their daughter, Lavinina, and son, Vasili, have a house just outside Lakka, above the beach, on the road that winds up in the hills towards Vasilatika, where Pano is rebuilding his old family home.

Eight o'clock came and went in Spiro Petrou's bustling kafeneon. Nine o'clock came and went. I was about to clamber back up the hill when the door to the kafeneon swung open and Pano virtually bounded in. Spotting me, he beamed, put his hands in the air, fingers outstretched as though in amazement, advanced on me, grabbed my hand in those two huge, powerful pianist's hands, and grinned.

'Welcome home!' he said.

The urge to believe him was indescribable.

These balmy days continued right up until a few days before Christmas, when the Paxos myth reasserted itself with a vengeance. Unfortunately, it also reasserted itself the day I was due to meet Graham, newly arrived from London for Christmas, at Pat's house at the other end of the island. But in that brief respite I had this tiny kingdom to myself. There were daffodils and dwarf pink cyclamen out already, and I spent one incredible afternoon sitting on the cliffs at Vasilatika watching thermals turning into clouds far out to sea. That afternoon really was warm enough to start a suntan. I hadn't even thought about sunblock, and was startled two days later, barely a day or so before Christmas Day, to find that my forehead was beginning to peel.

By that time the Paxos winter was back, and it seemed almost as though an entirely different island had suddenly emerged from the sea. On that island, rain lashed through the olive groves almost constantly, making the landscape as gloomy as the English countryside in deep midwinter. People on this island travelled everywhere by car, and had to light huge olive wood log fires at night to beat back the cold. Much of the time was spent surviving: shopping when there was a break in the weather, cooking heavy winter meals, collecting firewood, washing clothes so that they had a few days to dry, stocking up on emergency stores, defending the property and its perimeter against the elements. On this new island, people slept late, played marathon games of Scrabble, read long novels and made sure that they brought enough wood indoors for it to dry out for burning two or three days later. Thunder boomed from various quarters, and lightning played funny tricks with the visibility through the trees. On Boxing Day, we decided to walk off the previous day's indulgences and were surprised by a sudden gale; we might as well have been walking through that carwash. As winter closed in over Paxos again, in fact, we might just as well have been polar explorers.

TWO

TEMPEST

'There are people . . . who find islands somehow irresistible. The mere knowledge that they are on an island, a little world surrounded by the sea, fills them with an indescribable intoxication. These born "islomanes" are the direct descendants of the Atlanteans, and it is towards the lost Atlantis that their subconscious yearns throughout their island life . . .'

LAWRENCE DURRELL, *REFLECTIONS ON A MARINE VENUS*

THREE THINGS DEFINE AN ISLAND. Its littoral, the contingency of land it shares with the sea; the unfathomable depths that surround it and give it its shape; and the journey to it from somewhere else, somewhere usually larger, whose dwarfing size gives its smaller sibling the piquancy that is the islomane's pure heroin hit.

Islands, I now realise, have featured in my fantasies since I was a child. They range from the mundane to the fantastic: from the small grassy mounds in the middle of a series of ponds hidden in private woodlands where I used to trespass to play as a child, to the Galapagos, 600 miles off the coast of Ecuador, home of the blue-footed booby, the giant land turtle, the cast of characters in a Kurt Vonnegut novel named after the islands, and the giant iguana that writer Annie Dillard dozed alongside one afternoon during a visit there.

In between there are, variously, the Isle of Sheppey, where my parents once owned a caravan, and whose gloomy resorts exert a strange pull that still draws me back there; Lundy and Saint Kilda, the latter forcibly evacuated early this century much as some Greek islands were during the Second World War; Fire, and Coney, two extremes of American vulgarity, the former a disappointment, the latter a magnificent deco playground in terminal decay; the Orkneys, glimpsed across the terrifying stretch of water that separates them from the tiny harbour at John O'Groats; Bali, where I dream of someday seeing a version of the gamelan monkey dance that isn't put on for tourists; and Kastelorizo, the furthest of the Dodecanese, Megiste to the mainland Turks a few miles away across the Aegean. A German diplomat I met at a party told me he and his family used to sail there each year from Rhodes. It seemed so far-flung I used it as a place to hide a character in a novel I published some years ago. It gained brief, if largely anonymous, publicity as the setting for Gabriele Salvatore's 1992 film, *Mediterraneo*, and I dream of sailing a caique single-handed into its harbour one day.

We came to this island thanks to a string of coincidences so slender a breeze could have blown us off course. A friend invited us to a garden party being thrown by a friend of theirs. We met a travel writer, Mark Ottaway of *The Sunday Times*, at this party, and asked him the question you naturally ask a travel writer at a party: so where do you go on holiday from choice? He said Paxos, and outlined all the reasons not to come to Paxos: the journey, the water shortage, the lack of facilities. We filed this information away in our minds. A few months later, at the beginning of October, we were talking each other into taking a last-minute cheapo holiday somewhere in the sun. We hadn't been away for over two years, and were about to book a package to Lesbos when we were warned that the resort's beaches were made of concrete. Graham spotted an ad in the *Observer* for last-minute holidays on Corfu and Paxos. That one little ad, five lines of display tucked away in the travel classifieds, changed our lives for ever.

A few days later we were on a morning flight from Gatwick to Corfu. There was drizzle over southern England, cloud over the Alps, searing sunlight above the sea between Italy and Greece. As we stepped out of the aeroplane at Corfu airport, the lemon glare of the sun made us squint and the heat pressed in like bandages.

A minibus took us to the ferry, a journey of perhaps ten minutes, passing the tourist developments at the end of the airport's sole runway, around the bay to the south of the medieval fort that defends Corfu town, past the elegant arcaded Liston, overlooking a small park where drinkers sit and watch people play cricket under the beating Greek sun.

A row of large white roll-on ferries, of the sort that ply to and from Piraeus, were lined up against the harbour in the town's crumbling Old Port. At least these monsters could weather the sort of storms Mark Ottaway had mentioned.

Tucked in alongside these monsters was the MV *Kamelia*, perhaps a fifth the size of the gleaming white superstructures lined up beside the quay. It was and remains perhaps 120 feet long, with space at the back for two cars or vans, and was at this time painted a scruffy orange and red. For more than a decade, the *Kamelia* was Paxos's lifeline to the outside world. It could call in at all three ports, although at this point she was boycotting Lakka because of a dispute between the captain and someone he didn't like in Lakka, and would set sail in virtually any weather. It had a permanent list to starboard from some mishap during its heyday perhaps sixty years earlier as a Nile cruiser, and bizarrely it had been retired to one of the friskiest sea passages in Greece, as we were about to discover.

Strangers, nervous and fatigued, we retired to a corner of the ferry's cabin, and waited. We had travelled to Greece just once before, a dull, hot fortnight on the uninteresting Cycladean island of Andros, and had yet to succumb to whatever it was that Grecophiles succumbed to. Our linguistic skills had barely progressed beyond pointing and smiling, and were not forced any further by a holiday deal in which we were chaperoned in English on every leg of the journey apart from the ferry from Corfu to Paxos. Buying a beer, and thinking that you should carry out the transaction in Greek, was a major embarrassment, although the weather was to save us from this. When furniture is beginning to fly around the cabin, few are able to buy or consume cans of beer.

28 ·

The toasty Corfiot afternoon cooled into one of those Greek autumn evenings that turn black without notice. The inky darkness surrounded the ferry and harbourside, bringing lights on in the town. Shortly after nightfall, the *Kamelia* weighed anchor and set sail for Paxos. As the lights of Corfu town slid away behind us, the old ferry seemed all the more vulnerable, although this is probably a psychological factor in any such departure. As we moved out to sea, we could glimpse the stars coming out through the cabin portholes, which were open to the night air. The yellowy electric light in the cabin made it rather homely, although, confusingly, still alien; any comfort found here would come in a foreign language bewildering to most Britons.

The journey from Corfu town, or Kerkyra, to give it its proper name, to the southern tip of the island, where ten miles of open sea lay between us and Paxos, was as boring as it normally is; ninety minutes of the *Kamelia*'s noisy old engines thrumming through the shallow waters between Corfu and the Greek mainland ten miles away. At the south-ern end of Corfu, just past the disco nightmare of Kavos, the shallow inland waters meet the outer Mediterranean, which shelves from a depth of around 60 feet maximum between Corfu and Greece to over two miles deep in the trenches south-west of Greece and Italy, a few miles off the west coast of Paxos.

After an hour and a half of the three-hour journey, we had grown accustomed to the motion of the ferry, the noise, and the smell. The wood-panelled cabin might have dated back to the 1950s or even earlier, with two lines of ancient banquette seating facing each other across small, fixed Formica-topped tables on the port side and another two lines of banquettes on the starboard. There was a tiny bar serving drinks and snacks to the fore, just beneath the wheelhouse. Greek women dressed entirely in black slept stretched out on some of the banquettes, while other islanders sat and talked or argued next to them. We few tourists in the cabin stuck out like nervous giraffes marooned among amiable pygmies.

I was sitting on a banquette seat with my back to a port-hole that had, like a good many other portholes on the ferry, either rusted or just jammed open. Nothing would close it, and I'd slung a jumper across my shoulders against the cool evening breeze. Graham sat on another fixed banquette seat across the table from me. The journey south to Kavos had led us, lulled us, to expect this calm wallowing motion to take us all the way to our destination. We were wrong. The following is narrated with the benefit of hindsight.

As the ferry to Paxos passes the southernmost tip of Corfu, it has to set a course diagonal from the mainland and head out towards the island. This takes it at right angles through the prevailing north-westerly currents. As the ferry engages the seas at right-angles, a little-known quirk of what might be Chaos Theory comes into play, making it yaw, roll and corkscrew in a particular rhythm with a set number of waves, the frequency and violence of these movements depending on the strength of the seas and wind. In good weather, standing by the wheelhouse of the *Kamelia* as she rounds the tip of Corfu and heads towards Paxos, you can actually count the waves and, sensing the roll of the ship, spot the ones that will produce the most violent motion. This dark October night on our first journey to the island, we weren't to know that the *Kamelia* was sailing into the tail end of a very ugly storm blowing from somewhere else in the Mediterranean.

The first slap of salt water on the back of the neck through the porthole I took as fair play. When you get on strange boats in strange seas, you have to expect that sometimes they will throw things at you. My first ever trip abroad had been through a winter gale from Dover to Ostend, on a day when storms kept the ferries in port for twelve hours because the seas were so rough, and only relented to let them ride out into rollercoaster seas where the stewards pulled the blinds down to stop us seeing the waves exploding over the bow. This memory reminded me to expect some airborne seawater during our journey. It didn't say anything about the volume.

The second slap of seawater on the back of the neck followed quite quickly, as the ferry slipped to the port side with the greased ease of someone falling over on black ice. Suddenly, I had one hand clenched on the edge of the banquette seat beneath me, the other on a paperback of John Cheever's short stories, I was looking up 45 degrees at Graham looking down at me, and the tops of waves seemed to be coming in through the porthole behind me and other portholes besides. This was not normal, but I volunteered that wide-eyed idiot grin of the individual who believes himself to be truly imperilled, and shared it with strangers who were only too happy to share it right back.

Moments later, the ferry shot down from the port side, rearing up on the starboard and giving people seated on the other side of the cabin a wet and nasty surprise. I was still holding on to the seat with almost as much force as I was the Cheever, but now I was looking down 45 degrees at Graham looking up at me. People and things were falling over, slipping the moorings of gravity; the man behind the small bar at the fore of the cabin swept what loose things he could embrace into cupboards, boxes, a small sink. I became aware of the Greek passengers waking up, glancing around, the meaningful eye-contact between island neighbours, the certainty that I could never decipher the import of these loaded glances between people who knew exactly what was happening to us. As the *Kamelia* slid back to port again, some of the tourists in the cabin started trying to stand up.

My sweater was already wet with seawater, although I remember mainly being concerned with trying to hide my embarrassment at this fact, wondering how to pass this off as fine, normal; that's okay, I get soaked to the skin on a regular basis. It's a hobby of mine, honest. In the meantime, a man and a woman, clearly a couple, had positioned themselves by the side of the sole exit from the cabin at the back of the cabin. She had her handbag slung around her neck, as though preparing for a spot of treading water in open sea during a storm at night. She and her partner were holding on to each other as though they were about to say goodbye for ever. Our miniature remake of *The Poseidon Adventure* was missing only Shelley Winters, and I was the guy who would hold the rope and help her make that fateful dive.

Out into the middle of the open sea between Corfu and Paxos, the *Kamelia*'s motion grew more and more frightening. While varied by the interaction of ferry, wind and wave, the yawing and rolling was growing even more violent. The husband and wife couple had inspired others to join them in the doorway, and they did indeed resemble the classic cross-section of society that film directors assemble as extras in disaster movies: desperate, exposed, freighted with their own fears and terrible secrets. The rest of us were beset with woeful imaginings, although it seemed preposterous to think that our lives were in danger. Who dies while going on holiday? (Plenty, but we were busy blocking that bad news.) The Greeks were tense but not about to share their misgivings, even if any of the rest of us foreigners could have understood them.

Much of the passage between Corfu and Paxos was devoted to holding on for dear life. Reading was impossible, as the book-holding hand was better employed gripping a part of the ferry that the other hand wasn't already holding on to, or grabbing inanimate objects that were moving around of their own accord. In the traditional moment of terror, a minute can take an eternity to pass. The hour or so it took us to pass through the storm between Corfu and

Paxos seemed to last as long as those fantastic rows of zeros that Stephen Hawking wrote about in *A Brief History of Time*. We might, indeed, have taken the eternity metaphor quite near the point where Professor Hawking and his colleagues expect time to start running backwards. Heaven only knew what was happening to the people on the top deck.

Towards the end of this watery white-knuckle ride, powerful beams of light began to saw back and forth across the bulging black seas outside the portholes. The Lakka lighthouse was whirling its two white arms out across the sea towards us, and I'm unable to recall this voyage without thinking of a line from a poem by Malcolm Lowry, 'the lighthouse invites the storm and lights it'. Far from reassuring us, the strafing white lights seemed to confirm that we were in the midst of some maritime emergency. We were, of course, unaware that these lights were coming from a land-based lighthouse: they could equally have been spotlights coming from a rescue ship closing in on us as we sank into the arms of the kraken. A dog-eared American paperback edition of the collected short stories of John Cheever would be our only gravestone. That, and a sopping red jumper. As the handbag-clutching crew by the sole exit to the cabin began to quake, we waited in our own terror for alarms to start going off. Something had to happen. And it did.

Suddenly, the flailing white lights ceased. Swung high on one particularly lively hike up the port side, the ferry slid back down and remained on an even keel. It was as though somebody had switched off a piece of hydraulic machinery. Somehow, the tremendous seas had been stopped. The ferry was moving forward through calm waters, and the small crowd by the exit from the cabin were unstrapping their handbags. A few actually seemed tearful with relief. People, Greeks and visitors alike, resumed conversations that had been abandoned during the storm. Strangers shared sighs of relief, sheepish grins, raised eyebrows. The *Kamelia*'s engines were quietening as the ferry slowed down. Not all of us knew it – we certainly didn't – but we were now inside the protective horseshoe of Lakka bay. In minutes we would be disembarking on dry land.

The storm had wrought an effect that we were to find out about only later on. The *Kamelia* entered, and stayed the night in Lakka bay, breaking the captain's blockade on the village caused by his personal enmity with the unknown villager. We were meant to have sailed four miles further south to the island capital, Gaios, three-quarters of the way down the east coast from Lakka, which sits at the northernmost tip of Paxos. The weather made the journey down the coast to Gaios dangerous, perhaps even impossible. Out in the teeth of the gale, with the *Kamelia* attempting to break-dance, her captain had made the decision to run for Lakka bay. Between them, the lighthouse and the storm succeeded in ending the blockade.

At least, that is how islanders interpreted events for us afterwards. Certainly, on all our other trips on the *Kamelia*, at least those made during the main tourist season, the ferry called in at Lakka after that. Feuds between sea captains and small parties, as well as between other parties – the feud between the old baker and the rest of the village was one to savour – are also part of the magic realism on an island where the truth is rarely allowed to get in the way of a good story.

We stumbled off the ferry into arc-lit chaos on what we now know as the jetty in Lakka harbour. Confused tourists milled around looking like refugees off a boat somewhere exotic during the Second World War. We certainly felt like it. A young woman who had spotted our confusion introduced us to the travel representative, George, who had driven up from Gaios to rescue us. He drove us to our villa at the other end of the island, zooming through olive groves that looked like spooky Arthur Rackham prints when illuminated by his jeep headlights. Flashing through this eldritch landscape, we felt exhausted, numbed, drained. Did it really take all this effort just to get to Paxos? How on earth could anywhere be worth such an ordeal?

The villa was the upstairs half of an island merchant's home up in the olive groves. The kitchen was large enough for a family to use as a communal space, the bedrooms neat, tidy, spare. The windows revealed little more than what a low-wattage bulb could illuminate among the branches of nearby olive and cypress trees. The gaps in the windows let in the noise of the wind soughing in the trees. Alarmingly, gaps in the floorboards let up minimal glimpses of household life below. We crept around warily and wearily, improvising what a we could of a meal from a food pack we'd ordered from home: scrambled eggs, baked beans and crackers, washed down with warm Greek white wine. It tasted like manna from heaven. Tiptoeing around the raw pine floorboards of the island's main, perhaps sole, tailor's home, we climbed into a large Victorian double bed, underlit by beams of light from a sociable evening downstairs in the tailor's parlour, and slid into a sleep like vertigo, prone but moving forwards, like an aeroplane dipping and turning through turbulence, giddy as a boat hefted up by and sliding down the other side of great waves.

· 35

THREE

HARVEST

T HE WORK UP HERE in the olive groves around Vasilatika is
largely silent, save for the small noises of the winnowing and picking, the sacking of the olives, the wind
soughing in the trees, the occasional call, comment or joke
between us. Sometimes, distracted, Pano, a church cantor,
sings old folk songs, in a lovely, melodious choirboy's voice.

We work at a leisurely pace, which I first thought was
Pano being soft on the English dilettante who had offered
to help with his olive crop. In fact, the work in the olive
groves follows an entirely different clock than the one I am
accustomed to following at home. Work, any work, in
Britain, in London, seems to be about weekly, daily and
hourly deadlines. Here on Paxos, we may have nearly half a
year to collect all the olives that fall constantly through

these steep wooded glades. The amount of effort is probably the same, but expended in different ways, for different durations, and in a way I have never worked before. Undoubtedly, it was the only job I ever took in which the work made me physically ill, literally nauseous, vomiting, after the first day.

My career as an olive harvester began inauspiciously, late one May evening in Spiro's kafeneon. The decor in Spiro's probably hasn't changed since the Colonels came to power. A wooden bench runs around the wall on three sides, facing the bar which takes up the fourth, back, wall. Two doors interrupt the bench. Formica-topped tables are placed at intervals around the walls, and aged but sturdy wooden chairs accompany the tables. A huge antique dining table that looks as though it weighs a ton dominates the centre of the room, and is covered in oilcloth. This is usually decorated with a vase of flowers from Spiro's garden behind the kafeneon, and is a collecting point for freshly caught fish, bread deliveries, post and newspapers. A hi-tech bug-zapper hangs above the table, and there's a television hoisted up in the south-easterly corner of the room controlled by a remote wielded by the villagers who hang out around Spiro's espresso machine and chew the fat. Untold numbers of *Karelia* cigarette smokers have rag-rolled the ceiling a light brown. The shelves behind the huge counter refrigerator house bottles of Corfiot kumquat liqueur and ancient cocktails that probably aren't manufactured any more. The walls are hung with line drawings of unspecified parts of Greece, and a picture of an aircraft carrier. There's also, incongruously, a picture of Captain Pugwash and his crew aboard their vessel, and an old, old map of Greece and its islands, on which Paxos itself has been slowly erased by the untold years of people pointing and explaining. In the one place where you might locate the island's heart, it no longer exists. The coloured ink on the map has been rubbed away, leaving raw white paper that has dirtied over the years. The scar covers Paxos, Anti-Paxos, and a little bit of the mainland as well. If we could hear the words that have soaked into this map, this wall, over the decades, the most recurrent would be, 'Where are we?' and 'Here!'

We were sitting under the map this evening, enjoying an after-dinner Metaxa and Coke. Panayiotis joined us for coffee. As well as rebuilding his family home in Vasilatika, Pano still harvests his family's olive groves. As a young man, Pano served in the Greek merchant navy for many years. He travelled the world, and speaks the best English among those of his generation on the island. His English was gleaned from A5 crime comics, of the sort you used to find in old-fashioned sweetshops, translated with the help of a Greek-English dictionary. He can still come out with some of the phrases he memorised from the comics, gangster-movie clichés that propelled the four-frames-a-page narratives along. This particular evening, Pano was explaining how difficult it was to find help to gather his olive crop.

Two or three drinks west of reason, I said, 'I'll give you a hand.' This offer invited and received much merriment from around the table, especially from those aware of my aversion to hard work. Pano was amused, but played me along while others averred that I might faint under the weight of a jar of cocktail olives. Those two or three drinks became particularly insistent, defensively so, citing class background, worker solidarity, and worse. Grinning, Panayiotis told me to be at Vasilatika at eight the next morning, and everyone except me went home expecting that to be the last of it. We weaved our way home up the hill under the stars to bed, and Panayiotis went home probably expecting to spend the next morning working alone in his olive groves.

Brought awake by a blinding flash of memory and embarrassment at six the next morning, I rehearsed the previous evening's conversation – socialist comradeship and all – with Graham, who was awake in his bed next to mine. I asked, candidly, 'Am I behaving like a complete bourgeois dickhead?'

'Yes,' he replied, falling back to sleep.

I had two choices: stay in bed and become the butt of olive-picking jokes for as many summers as the witnesses to the previous evening's events cared to torment me, or go through with it. There was only one humane option. I dressed in shorts, T-shirt and sneakers, and slipped down to the village, seeking sustenance for the trials ahead of me: water, 7-Up for refreshment and enlivening sugars, and a few medicinal beers for later. Spiro Aronis, who sold me these things, later reported that I reeled through Lakka looking sick enough to die.

Apart from the two shops and the kafeneon, the village was silent as I passed through. Only the habitual early risers and day-long sunbathers were stirring in the apartments and villas around Lakka. A few villagers were about, glimpsed briefly in the alleyways and squares, but the only noise was that of cockerels, songbirds, distant goat bells, wind in the trees, the rattle of halyards at the quayside.

· 39

The walk to Vasilatika is one of the loveliest on the island. The concrete roadway gives out only a few hundred yards from the village, turning into a rutted mud track, returning to concrete again the two times it passes through small hamlets up in the hills. While the olive trees are everywhere up here, unlike the rocky and barren south of the island, the land beneath them is untamed, left to run to tall grass grazed by goats, carpeted with tiny pink cyclamen in the spring and again in the autumn. Some of the island's ninety-three churches are marooned up in these grassy hillsides, sometimes just a chapel, a small fenced-in churchyard, and perhaps a cracked and weathered bronze bell from the 1870s hung from a sturdy olive bough near by, still tuned and liable to give a rich, sonorous sound at the slightest tap of a fingernail. Ring one of these things properly on anything but a feast day and you'd start a civil defence exercise.

Approaching Vasilatika, the road overlooks some of Paxos's steepest valleys and out across the hills above Lakka. Paths lead off it to the former island capital, Magazia, up to the towering cliffs at Erimitis on the west coast, and down through thick scrub to the island's sole sandy beach, below the lighthouse. Vasilatika comprises just three houses, inhabited only occasionally, perhaps the same number of ruined medieval hovels, an ancient olive press, hundreds of years old, its wheel and wooden screw mechanism lying in the grass that grows within its roofless walls, and the abandoned remains of a more recent olive press, one that Pano remembers working in as a child. Madly, we once thought about buying this building, imagining its interior cleared and sunlight streaming in, the circular mill retained and put to some other use, cheery yellow light in the windows on still spring nights when we would sit outside and watch the fireflies cruising through the olive groves looking for love. The quoted price doubled as soon as we expressed interest, and all of a sudden the deal did not include any of the surrounding land. Given the foolhardiness of the project, we remain eternally grateful for the sobering effect of that price hike.

At 500 feet above the west coast, Vasilatika is one of the highest points on the island, and certainly the highest village or hamlet. There are one or two new villas planted with scant regard for the island skyline on some of the higher west coast clifftops, but these are recent developments, built with crude flamboyance by rich visitors. Simply connecting these properties to services – roads, electricity, water – makes them the most expensive on the entire island. The owners increase the sale value with swimming pools and campy movie-star architecture. I have been inside a few of these properties, and they felt like soulless, windy boxes. Whatever domestic comforts that might make them feel like home would have to arrive in the owner or visitor's baggage, for they were devoid of the personal belongings, knick-knacks and treasured possessions that make a place feel like someone's home, even if it is only a holiday home. As for the view, beyond the breathtaking first few seconds, when the visitor sways, stunned, and gulps in the view, the drama palls. Uninterrupted seascapes, while pretty, quickly become boring. Unlike residents of those properties with views of Corfu or the mainland beyond the east-coast waters, the inhabitants of these oceanic eyries are land-locked versions of Coleridge's Ancient Mariner, alone on his wide, wide sea.

For hundreds of years, Vasilatika shunned its sea view, crouched down the hill a way, below the treeline, in fact below the landline, away from the eyes of passing ships. As is suggested by its main structure, a fortified home and chapel with slits in the walls for riflemen to use in times of attack, Vasilatika has had reason to tuck itself out of sight of both the sea and the navigable tracks across the island. People have been living in Vasilatika since the fourteenth century, and perhaps earlier, and there is evidence to suggest that it was used as a refuge or hiding place when the island was overrun by invaders, be they Ali Pasha, Barbary corsairs, the Venetians, the French, the Russians, the British in the nineteenth century or Italian and German fascists in the twentieth. It is surprising that the Nazis found the village when they invaded the island, but they did. The Vasilatika olive oil had to be pressed in secret and smuggled down the cliffs, down frighteningly steep tracks and steps, some still visible from the sea today, to be hidden in caves just above the waterline. Pano's mother was one of the smugglers.

Nowadays, Vasilatika is visited mainly by adventurous walkers, or those few who have business there, like the retired sea captain who owns the second biggest house and the disused olive press that we tried to buy, and Pano, who visits during the olive season and outside it as well, when he works on the gradual renovation of his family home for his daughter Lavinina.

He was pottering about the the semi-ruined house when I arrived sweating and swaying after the half-hour walk from Lakka. He is in his early fifties, handsome, weathered, with a body that seems to be composed of pent-up kinetic energy, and a fondness for practical jokes that means he can never be entirely trusted. He was beside himself with amusement at the sight of me staggering into his garden, but wasn't about to turn down the offer of help, however feeble it might be.

Pano's family house is linked to another, his aunt's, in a odd little sunken alley that leads off the steep path rising into Vasilatika. The two houses look up through the olive groves to the wall around the Vassilas property, perhaps 50 yards away up a jumble of ancient stone terraces. All around are large, aged olive trees and pines whose vertical lines give the steep hillsides the air of a tall, spacious church. Over the wall are the giddying cliffs of the west coast, covered in gorse that clings tenaciously to a scree of stones and dirt that tumbles at an angle perhaps five degrees off the 90 degree upright down to the west coast. About a quarter of the way down the cliffs turn sheer, slicing straight down into deep blue-black water around the caves and sea stacks. A hundred yards or so out to sea a huge slab of rock juts out of the waves, either a massive rock-fall from the cliff face or a geological aberration in the tectonic upheavals that created Paxos. The slab, a few hundred feet of pitted and worn lime-stone hefted out of the sea like a contemporary sculpture installation, is home to hundreds of diving birds and shel-ters caiques that hover nearby hoping to net the shoals of fish that run in the area. From a perch on Pano's dry-stone wall, the bobbing ships look the size of toys. The view out over the west coast from Vasilatika is reminiscent of the hazy, mythic vistas of the paintings of Lawrence Alma-Tadema, minus the young women in their classical garb and the beautifully painted marble. As you stare down from Vasilatika at the Ionian glinting and flashing on a cloudless sunny day, those ancient mornings don't seem so very long ago at all.

There is another text at work here, of course, detailing the labour that must have gone into the stone terracing, the walls and the individual well-like terraces built around some of the trees. The invading Venetians, who protected the islanders from other marauders and won their support to the extent that Paxiots fought for them in their wars, paid the equivalent of a penny for each tree that was planted. There's an even older island buried here, the one that existed before a quarter million olive trees were planted on it. This would have been a feudal culture, or as feudal as life got on this small outpost of *demos* and *krasis* during the Renaissance. There is a church at the other end of the

· 43

island that is believed to have been built in the sixth century AD, but little else remains of medieval Paxos. On Halki,
Rhodes's nearest neighbour in the Dodecanese, there is a
medieval settlement built outside what is now a ruined
Crusader castle. The 'houses' are little more than sheep
pens with rock roofs. It's difficult, if not impossible, to imagine life in Vasilatika in those times, still less what the
hamlet looked like. Yet it's very likely that the planting of
the olive trees, along with self-propagating evergreens and
deciduous trees, bonded the island's top soil and probably
saved its life, giving the Paxiots a source of income for as
long as the olive trees survived. (They can live to be over
1,000 years old.) Each olive grove, each glade and hillside
and dell, is a miniature rock Machu Picchu. The work that
went into them remains as an imprint, although like the
eroded image of Paxos on the map in Spiro Petrou's kafeneon it is slowly beginning to disappear. A new generation
is turning away from the olive groves, leaving the work to
badly paid Albanian labourers, and here and there in the
olive groves the terraces are beginning to unravel.

Despite all the stone engineering on view in Vasilatika,
the evidence of man's civilising hand on crude rock and
stone, for me the olive groves here are a place at the end of
the world, somewhere cut off from the ferries that dock two
miles away, the aeroplanes that land and take off perhaps
thirty or forty miles away at Kerkyra, away from the books
and the laptop computer in my draughty room here, away
from the cultural profile that dogs me. I have stood on some
fastnesses before – in the strong landward winds of Land's
End and John O'Groats, for starters, but also the mountain-
top ruins of Monte Alban in the Sierra Madre del Sud, the
pyramids of Chichen Itza and Uxmal in the Yucatan, the
giddy pinnacle of the ruined Crusader castle on Halki, and

I've watched twilight fall and the stars come out from a canoe floating in a lagoon in a mangrove swamp on the edge of the Pacific – but none has had the magical effect that these trees at Vasilatika have on me.

The view from Pano's dry-stone wall is like a secret garden, a sudden, spectacular revelation waiting on the other side of the wall while we toil away in the olive groves. The work is slow, methodical, repetitive, hypnotic, but rarely boring. The eyes and motor facilities concentrate on the winnowing, picking out leaves, twigs and other foreign objects, sieving, picking more leaves and foreign objects out, sieving again, and transferring the olives to the thick grey plastic sacks that contained the fertiliser that islanders use as feed for the olive trees. While carrying out this motor function, the mind is free to wander, meditate or slip into sleep mode. On my first day in the olive groves, it took me a morning to winnow and sieve just one sackful of olives. With experience, or with Pano's deft fingers, that workload could double or even triple. In a normal year, one tree will yield perhaps four sackloads in one month. In an average year, each tree will be harvested on average around twenty-four to twenty-six times. This year, following the abnormal fruiting the previous year, and after the storms of November, the average is down to as low as six times. Pano works as though there is all the time in the world. We move from tree to tree, net to net – and each tree has at least three or four nets around it – tugging at the corners of the nets, piling the black gleaming fruit into an ill-assorted mound of olives and arboreal debris in the centre, plucking out the waste, winnowing, sieving, bagging, moving on.

The hands quickly take on a gooey purply-blue patina, as do any other parts of the body or clothing that they touch or that come into contact with the fruit. During a day's work, sundry itches, scratches, ticklish bits and rearrangements of clothing distribute this revolting residue around most of the accessible parts of the body, although the worst washes off quickly with water, leaving a purple stain on flesh and clothes. The oil must have a wonderful effect on skin and blood; on that first day alone, I must have absorbed enough oil by osmosis to pass muster as a self-basting turkey. In warm or clement weather, it's possible to clean off the goo and sweat by going for a swim during the siesta, or taking an outdoor shower in the sunshine. But as winter closes in, the workers in the olive groves grow dirtier, and smellier.

The rough plastic nets feel like sandpaper, and easily cut and scrape fingers and palms. The nets are an innovation of the last decade or so; prior to that the olives were brushed by twig brooms and scooped up by hand. In fact, Paxos and the nearby mainland region of Epirus seem to be among the few olive-growing regions which wait for the olives to fall to the ground rather than picking them when ripe. And even in Epirus the trees look younger and smaller, planted in rows like vineyards, and severely pruned to keep them at a manageable height.

In the centuries prior to the introduction of the nets, the island was swept, almost literally, from north to south, the ground beneath the olive trees cleared so that the olives could be collected by hand and basket. The only truly onerous task is the bending and squatting. As farmworkers through history have known, the human body was not designed for this work. An ideal creature for these tasks would have very strong arms that reach the ground, and very short and powerful legs. It would probably resemble a baboon. This ergonomic shortcoming among humans has resulted in terribly stooped backs among some of the older men and women on Paxos, some bent so bad they could be classified as crippled. On my first day in the olive groves, the bending and squatting produced dizziness and nausea, although these were probably exacerbated by the heat and a generous hangover. After a while, the strain begins to show in aches in thighs, hips, back, shoulders and arms.

Unlike work in Britain, however, here in the sighing wooded cathedral of Vasilatika there is always tomorrow to finish a sack of olives, always time to stop to take a break, drink water, talk, walk away and look at something that catches your eye. The pace prevents the Paxos olive pickers from developing the repetitive strain injuries that British workers get from performing rigid sets of movements – in food-processing plants and other factories, on computer keyboards – at the high, machine-like speeds that British management demands from them. Work in these olive groves may be dumb, filthy and badly paid, but it is work for humans, on a human scale.

Almost every family, and in the larger, dynastic island families, every branch of that family, will have some involvement in work like this. Many live in their houses up in the olive groves, and constitute a greater proportion of the island population than the people living around the three sea ports. Depending on the structure of each family, its wealth, and the age, number and gender of its members, each will have worked out how best to work its olive groves. It's often more lucrative, for example, for Pano's son, Vasili, to step into his father's shoes as the main village taxi driver than help in the olive groves. Unusually, Lavinina will sometimes help her father in the groves. She is the only young woman I have ever seen working in the olive groves. Marianthi, Pano's wife, stays at home, but not entirely as a traditional housewife; she is also the radio controller for this family-run minicab firm, contacting her husband or son on a squawking CB radio set wherever their work takes them on the island. Lavinina has her own small hairdressing business, set up for her by her parents to ensure her independence and her economic worth in a culture that still operates something like a dowry system. (She has since met, and become engaged to, a wealthy showbusiness photographer in Athens. However, like her brother, she still intends to return to Paxos.)

As we slowly work around the Vasilatika olive groves, Pano and I fill sacks with olives, tie them, and stack them outside the small gate, ready for collection. In an earlier time, in Pano's childhood, we would have carried them across the road to the sea captain's now-derelict olive press, where barefoot children, Pano among them, their mothers, and sundry animals laboured on the dirt floor to keep the millstone circling evenly around the olive mill. Then, other families in the Vasilatika area would also have brought their olives to the mill, a chore which led those too poor to afford a donkey, cart or truck to stagger through the olive groves under weights of olives that would eventually give them permanent curvature of the spine.

In an even earlier time, the olives would have been carried to the primitive stone hut on the perimeter of Pano's olive groves, built to serve the olive trees when they were first planted by the Venetians. The dimensions of this olive press suggest that its builders were a smaller race than modern-day Greeks and northern Europeans. These derelict olive presses that can be found across the island are crumbling memorials to the central role of olives and their oil in the island's life for hundreds of years. The olive trees and their fruit kept island and islanders alive through those centuries, when many Aegean islands became dusty, inhospitable rocks in the middle of the sea. Greece's islands and coasts were extensively deforested in ancient times to build first its own fleets and then those of its invaders. Britain's Crusaders sailed to the Holy Land on Greek wood. Byzantium and the Barbary corsairs fought sea battles on Greek wood. Marauding Turks and Russians went down to the sea on Greek wood. Their impact on the Greek ecology, combined with that of livestock such as goats allowed to roam free, can be seen on the bare brown hills of Epirus, lying on the eastern sea horizon like a family of bears curled up and asleep. The difference between the low hills of Paxos, where armies of olives and pines march down to the beaches like triffids massing for an attack, and the barren mainland is remarkable. The difference is quite literally the difference between life and death, and the sole factor in that difference is the olive tree and its oil.

For all the filth and noise and discomfort, what the olive press produces looks like something approaching nectar, a luscious, rich golden liquid, full of light and hints of forest green. Homer's Greeks seemed to have all manner of exotic uses for these oils, uses which modern man has forgotten. They – or at least the aristocrats Homer wrote about – oiled themselves after baths, and had various religious, social, medicinal and aphrodisiac uses for olive oil. Nowadays, its uses are almost exclusively culinary.

In truth, I only managed to help out a few times this olive season: the huge storms of November brought most of the crop down while I was in London, recuperating from an accident, leaving Pano to winnow and sort the remaining crop piecemeal through the winter. Yet is is intriguing to think where all this viscous wealth ends up. Oil from the olives I harvest in Vasilatika embarks on a culinary pilgrimage. It could turn up in delicatessens and kitchens in New York, London, Paris, Rome, Hong Kong or Sydney. It's taken home to Britain, Germany, Norway, Ireland, Canada and the Caribbean. It leaves with flotillas to spend the summer circling the Ionian, or the Med, feeding a thousand salad dressings and binding untold hundreds of fried eggs. It finds its way into the north-European food industry – baking, pre-cooked meals, gourmet foodstuffs, mass catering at all levels. It sits in friends' kitchens, a present from Paxos, used sparingly for special salads or cooked meals (you haven't roasted potatoes until you have roasted them in Paxos olive oil). It has been carried off by the round-the-worlders who have sold their homes, bought a yacht and sailed away, mooring for a few days in Lakka harbour and promising, as some have done, to sail back into the bay in a year or two from now to visit Lakka again. At this very moment, they could be using my oil to sauté potatoes while moored off Alaska, making a vinaigrette in the Galapagos, frying sausages in the Antarctic or mixing a mayonnaise in some paradisical Balinese cove.

In the lonely groves of Vasilatika in late autumn, midwinter or early spring, with an evening breeze rising and a weak sun sinking early in the west, sending shafts of light through the trees, shafts of light that tip up and up as the sun disappears below the cliffs and into the sea, this all seems amusing and odd to contemplate. In the darkness and silence of winter, it can sometimes seem that Vasilatika has fallen off the edge of the world. As shadows slip down from the crowns of the trees, it can feel like a place that has been utterly abandoned.

Yet beneath all this silence and shadow, in roots and trunks and branches, the biennial olive crop is developing in every olive grove, on every tree, for almost every family and individual on the island. Their cycle may have been sent out of kilter by environmental factors, but these sturdy olive trees are nature's answer to the perpetual motion machine, and have been blossoming and fruiting since the 1380s, the time of Wat Tyler and the Peasants' revolt, the reign of Richard the Second, and decades before the burning of Joan of Arc. And at every stage of the process, it has meant sustenance, employment and income for the islanders, all of it thanks to forward-thinking invaders from Venice.

And six centuries on, it is still happening. Every two years the trees react to a chemical in their root system and a subtle shift in climatic conditions and begin a process of fruiting which will produce this viscous liquid wealth. They will already have taken the precaution of producing a fake fruit the previous year, to trick predators and conserve energy, a crop of small, bitter olives that no one will harvest. If the rains are sufficient, the winter frosts light, the spring wet and the summer clear and warm, then the Paxiots can bank, quite literally, on another two years of olive oil and income. If the olive crop is threatened in any way, however, the island's economy could be jeopardised for the next two or three years.

Legend has it that mainlanders considered the Paxiots to be foolish island hicks, people who tried to join Anti-Paxos to its larger sibling by throwing a rope around it and attempting to pull it across the sea, people who threw buckets into wells at night to rescue the moon when they looked down and saw that it had fallen in. Yet here they are, 600 years since the death of Chaucer and still growing money on trees.

FOUR

ISTORIA

Despite the attentions of any number of unwitting publicists, from Plutarch to Mills and Boon author Anne Weale, Paxos remains Paxos thanks largely to its distance from history. Nothing famous was built or left to posterity on Paxos. No famous people were born on Paxos, and no famous events happened on or near Paxos. Where all manner of things – treasure, temples, battle sites, amphitheatres, sybils and oracles, mountains, ravines, architectural schools, ancient festivals – drew the eighteenth-century travellers who would blaze the trails that mass tourism has followed, Paxos remained on the sidelines. Until recent years, a conspiracy of travel writers preserved its obscurity, and even encouraged people to confuse it with similar-sounding islands. Paros and Naxos are regularly misheard for Paxos, and the conspirators do nothing to correct the confused, either; they are happy, in fact, that this unwanted attention has been deflected away to the other side of Greece. Some will go to great lengths to keep Paxos hidden. In his *The Greek Islands*, published in 1978, Lawrence Durrell dismissed Paxos and Anti-Paxos as 'two islands of little note', although he may have had his own less-than-honest reasons for this casual damnation. Durrell couldn't have spent the time on Corfu described in *Prospero's Cell* without having at least heard about the charms of Paxos. His brother Gerald was a regular visitor for decades. I suspect he was helping to preserve a well-kept secret.

Yet it would be wrong to think that history caught Paxos taking a nap. The island may be off the track beaten by the guide books and the coach parties, but it has been around for a couple of major events in Greek history, and even had a walk-on part in a historic moment in the development of western civilisation.

One of the first pieces of Paxos mythology that the visitor learns concerns the story about Paxos, or perhaps Erikousa, as it was then known, and the death of the god Pan, the god of fields and woods, shepherds and flocks, who is most often figured as a man who has goat's legs, horns and ears, an image that lent itself to the Christian image of the devil. In his *Moralia*, Plutarch tells of an Egyptian sea captain, Thamous, who was sailing north through the Ionian, being becalmed between Paxos and the mainland. On their first evening in these doldrums, Thamous was on deck and heard a voice call out to him from the direction of Paxos. The voice told him that when he reached the port of Pilodus, opposite Corfu on the Epirot mainland, he was to shout out three times to its people that the great god Pan was dead. Thamous was reluctant to do this, but when his ship was becalmed again, off Pilodis, he decided to do as he had been told. A great wailing rose from the sea, followed by a wind that helped him on his way. The cheerful pagan Lawrence Durrell dismisses the possible connection, but the myth is popularly linked to the death of the old, pagan world and the beginning of the new, Christian world.

A hundred or so years before Plutarch wrote this, in 31 BC, Paxos made its first and still rather apocryphal appearance in history, as the place where Mark Antony and Cleopatra dined on the eve of the battle of Actium, where their fleet was defeated by that of the Emperor Octavian under the leadership of the Roman general Marcus Agrippa. The battle of Actium brought the dazzling careers of Antony and Cleopatra to an abrupt end, although it is not known if their last meal before the battle contributed to this. Yet the 'Cleopatra's dinner' story has launched a million and one tourists' jokes about greasy moussaka and cold chips. Surprisingly, no-one has yet opened a taverna or bar themed on the event.

The island also has its own small place in mythology, although that, too, is open to if not doubt then disagreements over interpretation. It is generally accepted among mythologists that the island was created by Poseidon, who struck the sea with his trident, the emblem of Paxos and the other six islands that form the Ionian archipelago, the seven islands known, in literal Greek, as the Eptanisa. In one version of the story, Poseidon was looking for somewhere to hide his wife Amphitrite, and so created Paxos. In another, he wanted somewhere to rest between Corfu and Lefkas (rather odd, given his superhuman powers; Homer writes about other deities traversing the entire Mediterranean with ease) and so created an Olympian motorway services layby ten miles south of Corfu.

It also features, semi-officially and unofficially, in the Odysseus/Ulysses myth, although this is largely unfounded. It has been estimated that Odysseus's time at sea would make Corfu a likely spot for him to have washed ashore and been discovered by Nausicaa and her handmaidens. Historian and explorer Tim Severin actually cites Paxos in his book about his reconstruction of the epic voyage, *The Ulysses Journey*, and even suggests that Lakka bay, probably Harami beach, is the place where Ulysses was washed ashore, and where his men saw the smoke from Circe's home and made the fatal decision to seek the help of whoever had lit the fire. There are also some curious coincidences of naming around Paxos itself that lend themselves to the myth. A small valley near Ipapanti is known as Circe's Grove, after the woman who imprisoned Odysseus and his men, turning the latter into pigs. Superstitious islanders tend to give this place a wide berth. And one interpretation of Moggonissi, the island to the south of Gaios, is Pig Island. Severin's theory is at variance with a number of classical interpretations of the myth, but it does have one key piece of evidence in its favour: Odysseus's visit to the gates of hell to commune with the dead took him to the River Acheron, which runs into the Ionian directly opposite Paxos, and is known, locally and in history, as one of the rivers running into the Styx. He also has some pretty convincing arguments for siting Scylla and Charybdis on Lefkas and its neighbouring mainland, 50 kilometres south of Paxos.

It is generally now accepted, as the title to Durrell's famous slim volume of life on Corfu in the year running up to the Second World War attests, that Corfu is the imagined site of Prospero and Miranda's cell in Shakespeare's *The Tempest*. As Durrell says, Corfu and Paxos were well known to the Elizabethan intelligentsia. Indeed, Corfu and, to a lesser extent, its southerly neighbour, have both been stop-off points for artists who have travelled in the region. It is thanks to Edward Lear that we have images of nineteenth-century Paxos, including Gaios and Lakka, from a time when the latter comprised little more than a few huts on the seashore. As a lamp post on the main beach suggests, prior to the construction of the harbour the village's boats would probably have run themselves aground on the beach (a suggestion made stronger by the presence of the path to the beach, a path that was there decades before the first tourist's flipflops trod it). It is also possible that this tradition actually helped create the clear sandy bottom just below the waterline; a painting in Spiro Petrou's kafeneon also lends itself to this suggestion.

By the time Edward Lear began producing images of Paxos, in his collection of watercolours and sketches from the years he spent on Corfu and travelling the Ionian, the topology and vegetation of the island would have been established more or less as we know it today. The Venetians arrived in the fourteenth century, and initiated their plan of olive planting and civic construction shortly afterwards. It is hard to imagine what Paxos looked like before the Venetians arrived, although the sleepy brown bears of the nearby mainland may give us an idea of how it might have looked and how it might have ended up had the Venetian olive afforestation not taken place. At one point in prehistory, when the upper half of the Adriatic was in fact dry land, Greece and its neighbouring territories were covered by the great Tethys Forest.

Torrential winter rains have kept Paxos's olive trees alive for over 500 years and nourished the evergreens, deciduous trees and innumerable shrubs and plants that burst out across this deep green island each spring. Whatever the unhappy aspects of Venetian rule – and there must have been some, although in a region regularly overrun by pirates and invaders, the Paxiots, like the Corfiots, actually sided with their Venetian rulers – the happy accident of reforestation kept the island's ecology on an even keel, and one that would only be disturbed by the beginnings of tourism.

This green island first appears in the history books around 300 BC, when it was recorded as the site of a great sea battle off the island, fought by a Corfiot warrior queen and her navy against an Illyrian army. At this time, Paxos, like the rest of the Ionian and surrounding territories, was under the rule of the Roman Empire. (I am indebted to the Paxiot writer and historian Yianis Doikas's book, *Paxos: History, Folklore, Culture*, for this information.) It remained under Roman rule until the eighth century, by which time Paxos was already settled and boasted at least one church and harbour at Ozias. In 733 it became one of the outposts of the vast Byzantine empire. Ten years later it fell under the despotic rule of Epirus and its leader Ali Pasha. Fifty years on it was overrun by French, probably Norman, invaders, who were themselves supplanted by Venice in 1386. The Venetian rule lasted more than 400 years, until the region fell to the French again in 1797. This rule was brief, however; two years later the Ionian and surrounding territories were swept by the Russo-Turks, though they were forced to relinquish the region back to the French in 1807. The French ruled the region for more than a century, until aggressive action by the British military brought the Ionian under a largely benign English rule. The English ceded the archipelago to Greece in 1864. By this time, however, the island's population had been removed, erased, driven off or killed by sundry famines, pogroms, and forced or voluntary evacuations on numerous occasions. After one such disaster, it was estimated that barely 500 Paxiots remained alive on the island. Through this violent editing of the Paxos genealogy, only a few of the original families remain of those who gave their names to the island's early settlements.

Paxos remained under Greek rule until the German and Italian invasion of Greece in 1941. The Nazis, who finally took over the Ionian, were particularly cruel to Paxos, confiscating the oil crop and, according to one account, using Lakka bay as a target for practice bombing runs by German aircraft. The claim that an Allied submarine spent part of the war hiding in the sea caves of the west coast, sneaking out at night to sink enemy craft, has largely been discounted as another part of the mythology. The first time I came across the tale, being enthusiastically embellished by Yiannis Grammatikos from behind the wheel of his sea taxi as it bobbed in the swell below Vasilatika, it was obvious that Yiannis was doing this to annoy a group of German tourists who had unwisely stepped aboard his sea taxi that morning. Stratis Haviaras's novel, *When the Tree Sings*, set on an unspecified Aegean island, gives a vivid account of what the Nazis did in Greece (just as his later *The Heroic Age* goes some way to explaining what happened during the Civil War). While the Nazi depredations on Paxos may have been petty and vindictive, it also seems to be the case that the island spent much of the war unaware of what was happening in the wider world. When the victorious British sailed into Lakka, the Germans, who had taken over the schoolhouse, tried to arrest them, until the British explained – with some delight, one imagines – that it was actually they who were being arrested.

The short-lived junta of the Colonels, from 1967 to 1973, barely affected Paxos, although visitors at the time remember the army patrols at the airports and the spot checks on the length of young men's hair. The islanders largely ignored whatever edicts the Athens regime handed out; by the time they got to Gaios or Lakka, or were discovered to have not been obeyed, the orders would have been out of date. Again, its distance from the whirring cogs of history kept Paxos out of trouble.

Recent decades, the fall of the Colonels, the shifts between PASOK and New Democracy governments – meaning, in a sense, Labour and soft Tory, on an island that has been dominated at local level by KKE politicians (meaning, really, Euro-Communism, with centre-left Labour policies) – might look something like Frances Fukuyama's 'end of history' theory, when all the Big Things that might have happened in history have happened, and in which Paxos joins the rest of the undeveloped world in a post-modern boundaryless global leisure industry distinguished solely by local incidental details of language, culture and landscape.

This might appear to be the case in high season, late July and through August, on nights when the rat packs are running in Gaios, Loggos and Lakka, when the crowds of rich northern Europeans are elbowing their way through the streets, alleys and squares, wielding attitude and bad manners, when the atmosphere in the three harbour villages begins to resemble Blackpool or Southend or Margate on a sweltering 1960s Bank Holiday Saturday night, and when any caring deity would equip her or his subjects with powerful firearms and declare open season on the island's visitors. (Yes, including me. I'd know enough to stay up here in the garden until the carnage was over.) At these points, Paxos and Lakka begin to merge into every other overheated resort around this dying sea that has too many people corralled in too little space, all of them demanding a good time because they've paid so much for it. These are the times when I find myself reluctantly agreeing with writer James Hamilton-Paterson's claim (in his magnificent *Seven-Tenths*) that tourism can actually annexe islands to the mainland, effectively unislanding them. In the wild and noisy nights of the high season, Paxos really can begin to resemble a bar scene from Kurt Weill's *Mahagonny*, and at the moment before the apocalyptic storm strikes.

Away from the summer's peak, however, and even in the busier periods on either side of this season of heat and madness, the island evades conscription into this crazy, blurred future. Distance, bodies of water, that wide air and those rising thermals, ten miles of water that may well have saved untold numbers of lives, cut Paxos off from the end of history.

FIVE

 LIQUID GOLD

The whole Mediterranean, the sculptures, the palms, the gold beads, the bearded heroes, the wine, the ideas, the ships, the moonlight, the winged gorgons, the bronze men, the philosophers – all of it seems to rise in the sour, pungent taste of these black olives between the teeth. A taste older than meat, older than wine. A taste as old as cold water.

LAWRENCE DURRELL, PROSPERO'S CELL

T HE WORK IN THE ISLAND'S two modern olive oil presses is probably the hardest of the olive crop: the noise, dirt, smell and the handling of the sacks conspire to make this every bit as hellish as any heavy-industrial factory work in Britain. This labour is probably the most hated in the Paxos olive business, and it is this sort of work that younger islanders hope to avoid. An older, stone olive press still exists, near Magazia in the centre of the island, and is used fitfully to process a small family crop. It is opened mainly as a working tourist attraction – Paxos's first and so far only venture into the heritage industry. The modernised presses, in Lakka and Gaios, use mechanised equipment, breaking the rules that foodies insist produce the finest oils of Tuscany and the south of France, but the olive oil sold on Paxos is acknowledged to be among the finest in Greece.

After the effort it takes the islanders to produce it, it ought to be. Vasili Vassilas worked in the Lakka olive press this winter, and a pair of old, off-white jeans he wore to work quickly turned tar-black from the work. Spiro Aronis, the nearest I've encountered to a Greek separatist in the village and no stranger to the olive harvest himself, becomes particularly angry when visitors crack inane jokes about the olive harvest, usually condescending, as though this vital crop was no more than a Sunday afternoon blackberrying expedition in the countryside. 'It is not something to joke about,' he said grimly, the first and only time I ever made a quip about the olive crop, one autumn when the olive season was approaching. 'No,' he said, glancing at me darkly and then staring bug-eyed at a large cheese he was cutting behind his shop counter, as though transferring violent thoughts to an inanimate object, 'it is not something to make jokes about at all.' The earthquake weather that scudded across Spiro's brow at that moment was extraordinary: anger, resentment, bitterness – reasonable sentiments for islanders to feel towards their summer invaders – bulged and heaved just below the surface. For Spiro, the Paxos olive crop seemed to be something that yoked twentieth-century Paxiots to a medieval, peasant, past. I couldn't tell if his indignation was personal or general, although I could tell that he had had enough of the olive harvest himself. That September morning, I learned to handle Spiro Aronis with kid gloves.

After the olives have been winnowed and bagged, they are left by the roadside for collection by the olive press. The workers in the press, usually two labourers under a manager who tends the machinery, unload the olives into a sump resembling the pit in a commercial garage, which is the start of a conveyor-belt process that keeps the olives on the move until they finally emerge as virgin olive oil. They are winnowed for a final time at high speed, and then crushed in a machine which removes pits and skin which are ejected from an exhaust at the back of the olive press, producing the huge mounds of odorous, dusty pith that surround the factory. They are then passed through a mechanical washer, a long series of rollers semi-submerged in a constant stream of fresh cold water. The cleaning process is rarely smooth, and the olives have to be shoved back and forth to keep the process moving. This soup of pulped olives and water is ground into a rich and filthy brown mush, and then pumped into a centrifugal separator, the heavier olive oil draining out into the first of a series of settling tanks while the water, now blood-red and stinking from the residue it has picked up from the olive skin, is drained away into a large tank. From here it is pumped out into the sea through a pipe that extends out to the south-eastern side of the bay, just beyond the small jetty, where this organic and non-toxic waste stains the bay a bright pink-red, and, depending on currents and winds, can hang around for days at a time. Those who have accidentally swum into this report that the water can produce a sensation on the skin akin to mild burning. Depending on the weather and prevailing winds, it can also seed the air around Lakka with a faintly acrid smell, from the acids that are leached from the olives in the oil-making process.

This acidity may seem surprising for so smooth and oily a fruit, but the olive is an unusually unpalatable fruit raw. A member of the drupe family, it is one of the hardiest flora on the planet. How it came to be discovered, both as a fruit and as a source of oil, can only be imagined; nature designed the olive to deter anything with a digestive system as sensitive as man's. People often think that olives can be eaten straight from the tree. This is far from the case. The olives we buy in supermarkets and delis have to be washed in water and salt for up to forty days, with a change of water and salt each day, before enough natural acids have been leached from them to render them edible. The discoverer of the edible olive must have tried one that had fallen from the tree and been washed by the rain, a river or the sea, suggesting a certain desperation on his or her part. The invention of the domesticated olive is as mysterious as the invention of tea.

American author Maggie Blyth Klein, in her *The Feast of the Olive*, says that the olive tree, *Olea Europaea*, has been cultivated in the Mediterranean since prehistory. References to it, in the recorded word and in art, date back beyond 2500 BC, when the olive branch appeared in Minoan art works. In all probability, its cultivation dates back to before the recorded word first acknowledged it. Klein has tracked olive cultivation back to prehistoric Crete and Syria, where the olive culture appears to have developed independently of either site, and spread out across the Mediterranean with either traders or invaders. Beyond its culinary uses, olive oil has been used as medicine, a base for cosmetics, fuel for lamps, currency, and as a substance for anointing individuals in a wide variety of religious ceremonies. In Roman and Greek cultures, certain oils were the preserve of the social élites, others were abandoned to the lower orders. As a cultural symbol and metaphor, it forms a holy trinity of sorts with bread and water. No less a mind than Aldous Huxley described olive trees as 'numinous', divine.

Olive trees are believed to have been introduced to mainland Greece in the tenth century BC. Although the small green Ionian olive grows on Paxos, the olives harvested here are mainly olives from the Kalamata region in central Greece. These trees can live to over a thousand years. Like the starlight falling on Paxos, this olive oil has been on its way to us for hundreds of years.

When it emerges from the centrifuge, it already has the weird glow, a strange interior light, that we see when we bottle it. It really might be liquid gold. The oil is kept in 10-gallon drums, its source identified on the side, in a cannery opposite the olive press. It is left to settle, and tested at various stages for acidity, with the care usually reserved for wines or spirits. Some is given back to the individual families, depending on their requirements, for domestic use, and also as a form of barter, or gift. Much of the profit from the oil is made from sales on the island, through the olive presses and canneries, through the shops and restaurants, or even through individuals selling oil to visitors. Paxos oil costs about the same as some of the prime virgin press Italian olive oils. Unsurprisingly, whatever is left after these arrangements have been seen to is sold on to a company in Brindisi, on the south-eastern tip of Italy, where it is sold on into the European oil market as a blend 'Made in Italy'.

Workers emerge from the ramshackle one-storey olive press a different colour from the one they entered it earlier in the day. While the end product is pure, conditions around its place of production are not. Amazingly, smoking is allowed in both press and factory, and this Christmas the press acquired its own small Christmas tree, which was decorated with empty beer cans. The whole scene is dusted a dark tan by the dry residue of the pressing process, and in a low light the workers resemble the heroic figures from an American daguerreotype or sepia tint from the nineteenth century, like a scene from the goldrush era, which is apt. On paper at least, these people are millionaires.

SIX

THE STARS
OVER PAXOS

T HE NIGHT AFTER that first nightmare journey to Paxos, we spent the evening in Gaios and walked back to the tailor's house in the dark. Gaios was, and remains, a compact and pretty port, with a square abutting the harbour front, facing across to Aghios Nikolaos island, with its magnificent stand of pines that look as though they were drawn by Hokusai. There is a small church in the square surrounded by a guard of pink oleanders, and along one side of the square there is a small parade of tavernas and bars. The squares and alleys off it contain the village's dozen or so tavernas, none of them, if memory serves, very good. The whole place has the air of a miniature folly in the manner of Portmeirion.

Compared to Lakka, however, Gaios is Piccadilly Circus,

and some go out of their way to avoid visiting it, except to go to the island's one pharmacy, or perforce to visit the tiny magistrates court or police station. Peter Bull, the one time we met him in his garden in Lakka and asked if he'd care to visit us for a drink in Gaios, made it more or less plain that he was about as likely to take a stroll into Harlem alone at night as he was to visit Gaios voluntarily. Over the years we have found ourselves drifting towards a similar opinion, if only because Gaios has come to represent so many of the things – crowds, noise, money, snobbery, posing, attitude – that we come to Paxos to avoid. It is frightening to contemplate, but parts of Gaios, like parts of backstreet Corfu, are beginning to resemble a shopping mall.

That October night, however, Gaios in the late evening was quiet, shadowy, and nearly deserted. You could hear the sea lapping against the harbour front, the slap of halyards and the creak of boats along the quay, and there was very little noise from the bars or tavernas. We walked out of the village with torches that lit up small ovals of road surface ahead of us, but left the surrounding landscape pitch black and potentially full of any number of menaces: dangerous animals, maniacs with axes, dancing hobgoblins, worse. This was probably our first time in such natural darkness, although our apprehension eased as we slowly gained our nightsight.

68   The road out of Gaios is almost straight, with a few small kinks in it, until about a mile out of the village where it turns 90 degrees to head north towards Lakka. For part of the way it is hemmed in by low-rise apartments and then rocky hillside, but at one point, where a dry riverbed runs beneath the road, it takes a slight turn and the surrounding trees open out above it. It was at this turn, stopping to glance up, that I first saw God's blood streaming in the fir-

mament. The Milky Way appeared to have parked itself directly above and in line with the road in a way that you only see in Steven Spielberg movies. The stars were as big as golf balls, the white mist of the more distant stars inside the disc of the galaxy was a band of cloud you could almost reach up and touch, and the smaller stars on the periphery of the stream itself gleamed like Christmas decorations. The starlight was so bright it illuminated the olive groves, and after a short period of stunned gawping, terminated only because of chronic dizziness, we found we didn't need our torches any more. The night landscape of Paxos emerged in the manner of *la nuit Americain*, the *Day for Night* of Francois Truffaut's film, the cinematic device of filming 'night' scenes by using plain daylight without any additional lighting to get that atmospheric, film noir twilight. (As any number of British B movies from the 1960s will prove, *la nuit Americain* was also an extremely cheap effect to achieve.) It was almost as though we were walking through a photographic negative of the landscape, with a huge garland of lights strung overhead. It was impossible to watch the Milky Way for more than a minute or so before the dizziness set in again, and lying in the road, or even on the edge of it, is a dangerous thing to do at night on a one-road island like Paxos.

The Milky Way disappeared again after this turn, but still sparkled through the overhanging branches of the olive trees, and reappeared when gaps occurred in the branch cover. This pause became a nightly ritual, at least on nights when the sky was clear. I had, and have, never seen the stars so clear and so bright as over Paxos. Spending most of the time in a city where skyglow erases many of the features of the night sky, it is easy to forget about the extraordinary detail of the universe, and these dazzling points of light up above this tiny island served as a reminder of its presence, and might even be said to be the nearest an agnostic might get to having a religious experience. These swathes of nuclear hot-spots, zillions of miles away, bring a sense of mystery to the everyday (well, night). Writer Timothy Ferris has traced this metaphysical fascination with the stars back to ancient Greece and Egypt and beyond.

Certainly, they rekindled a personal interest in astronomy more or less dormant for more than a quarter of a century. An early devourer of books, I joined the junior library as soon as I was old enough and borrowed anything with pictures of dinosaurs, volcanoes, planets or stars. This was no precocious scientific intelligence, rather a lurid interest in the bizarre, the spectacular, and the violent. The interest in astronomy outgrew the dinosaurs and volcanoes, to the extent that I acquired a small telescope on a miniature tripod for Christmas at the age of ten or eleven. Well, with three older brothers, and considering early bedtimes, it took me two or three days actually to lay my own hands on the instrument. I built an observatory in the back garden from cardboard boxes, and entertained unscientific fantasies about constructing something in the garden involving a few bits of metal and a couple of batteries that would, somehow, send messages into outer space. ('Boy Communicates With Mars!' the newspaper headlines said in my imagination. The world press would beat a path to 19 Beddington Road, St Paul's Cray, Orpington, Kent. I would circle the Earth with the Martians in their flying saucer, stopping wars and bringing an end to world poverty by threatening to zap the superpowers. We would give them a little taster by barbecuing Moscow, or New York.)

But then, one boring afternoon a year or so later, curiosity got the better of me and I dismantled the telescope to see how it worked. Of course, I was unable to reassemble it, and quietly packed the pieces away in a corner of a cupboard. Shortly afterwards, I abandoned myself to the senseless pleasures of masturbation, furtive smoking and rock music.

A quarter of a century later, strolling up a hill on a small Greek island, my memory went rocketing back to that telescope, and the evenings spent lying in my duffelcoat out in the snow, telescope to the heavens, hoping for the odd supernova, perhaps, or a spacecraft with fins.

The stars over Paxos revived my interest in astronomy to the extent that, although I have not purchased another telescope – *yet* – I have acquired an expensive pair of East German binoculars, and am not afraid to look nerdy by travelling on public transport reading books about meteors or titles produced by that eccentric British institution, Patrick Moore. The binoculars come from a shop on Farringdon Road, based in the marvellously named Telescope House, just down the road from the *Guardian*. It is the sort of old-fashioned shop that might easily be the front for a secret organisation, like the cleaners that fronted the headquarters of UNCLE, and I wouldn't be at all fazed to find Mr Waverley serving behind the counter at Telescope House. It is crammed full of telescopes, some of which are ceiling-high, and could probably find you the sort of images of horsehead nebula and spiral galaxies that I drooled over in library books. Given an excuse, I cruise around Telescope House ogling the wares just as some men cruise car showrooms or sex shops. Unsurprisingly, I have daydreamed many a time of becoming wealthy enough to ship one of these monsters out to this garden, becoming Lakka's very own Tycho Brahe or Johannes Kepler at his viewfinder. I don't find telescopes sexy, but they exude a powerful magic, the ability to show you such fantastical, elemental sights, and at such distances that the act of viewing actually involves a journey back in time. Light years are measurements of distance, not time, but when involving observation they do also carry the coincidental information that this light has taken a certain amount of time to reach our eyes. Annie Dillard once described the sunlight in her Virginia valley as 'light from an explosion on a nearby star eight minutes ago', and even though the notion of light years has been a commonplace for decades, the idea that the light I am seeing from a star 'left', or was created by, a star in the past is something I find endlessly fascinating.

Take, as a random example, the constellation of Orion, the hunter. Betelgeuse lies 425 light years away from Earth; that is, 425 (light years) times 186,300 (speed of light per second) times 60 (seconds per minute) times 60 (minutes per hour) 24 (hours a day) times 365 (days per year) miles. Give or take a few inches, that works out at 2,496,941,640,000,000 miles. And Betelgeuse is comparatively nearby in the scheme of things. The light we see from Betelgeuse today left the star shortly after Queen Elizabeth I was crowned. The next brightest star in Orion, Rigel, is 1050 light years away. Light from there reaching us today left the star before the Norman Conquests. The next in magnitude, Bellatrix, at 360 light years distance, in the other shoulder to Betelgeuse, produced this light during the reign of Charles I. One could go through the entire constellation, the entire visible universe, matching stars to the historic events that occurred when they were producing the light we see now. The most distant star in the constellation, Iota Ori, a double star on the edge of the famous Orion Nebula that floats 'in' the hunter's belt, is 1900 light years away. When the light we see in this double star today left for Paxos, Vikings were still raiding Britain's east coast.

This also, of course, rather undermines the notion that the constellations actually fit the shapes we ascribe to them, the names we give them, and in terms of astrology, the psychological qualities this pseudo-science ascribes to the twelve signs of the zodiac. The stars in Orion, or in any other constellation, bear no physical relation to each other whatsoever, and are mere fanciful fictions dreamt up thousands of years ago, by Greeks and Arabs, largely, recorded by Ptolemy, marshalled into some semblance of order by astronomer royal John Flamsteed in the seventeenth century and given a numbering system still in use today by Charles Messier a century later. The naming and shaping of constellations is utterly arbitrary, as the images associated with just one constellation, Ursa Major, by different cultures suggest: Saucepan, Big Dipper, Bear, Drinking Gourd. If we had a place in another suburb of the galaxy other than the one where we are now, we might live under skies lit at night by such famous constellations as the Barbecue Tongs, the Proctoscope and the Television Detector Van. If they also have a California out there, it must be terrible indeed to introduce yourself to people at parties by telling them you're a Barbecue Tong, or, worse still, a Proctoscope.

Fittingly, while the Mayans perfected their calendar around 900 BC, and built the magnificent observatories at Monte Alban, Chichen Itza and Uxmal, it seems likely that the Greeks were the first to begin naming this universe of ours (even if the word universe itself has a Latin origin). The word planet derives from the Greek *planetes*, or wanderer, a reference to the motion of the planets through the night sky. Star, and asteroid, derive from the Greek *aster*, for star (although astral is Latin). Moon comes from the Greek *men*, and comet from the Greek *kometes*, for hair. It is ironic

· 73

to note that, despite the extraordinary achievements of the Mayans and early Greeks, possibly two of the greatest cultures the planet has seen, our knowledge of the universe is dominated by a Christian culture that has spent 2000 years stubbornly denying the simplest mechanisms of that universe, things that the Greeks and Mayans had worked out for themselves and incorporated into their pagan theologies. Indeed, the Mayan calendar, a beautiful but crude-looking thing comprising a circle of patterned abstract marks, was proved some years ago to be accurate to within a matter of a few seconds. Ancient Mexicans invented this device, along with hospitals, observatories and navigational equipment, at a time when the Europeans who would destroy their culture were still running around in the woods with no clothes on throwing rocks at each other. The dominance of the Christian ideology, which can still inspire a computer engineer to inform a writer that the universe was built by God within the last 10,000 years, is probably the greatest example of superior firepower in the history of warfare. Guns, and Crusader swords, won this universe for God, nothing else.

The mention of hair, *kometes*, leads me by the nose to the poetry of outer space. Astronomy is a science that flirts with the humanities, not least in its nomenclature. Just to the left of Ursa Major and down a bit is a cluster of some fifty or so stars known as Melotte III or the Coma Star Cluster. 'Behind' them, as it were, is the Coma Cluster of galaxies, a mere 250 million light years away by foot or bus. Of the fifty stars in this constellation, only one has a name, Diadem, the brightest, and only three others were reckoned worthy of inclusion in the *Collins Pocket Guide to Stars and Planets*. Yet this nondescript collection of stellar objects goes by the lovely name of Coma Berenices, or Berenice's Hair, a reference to Queen Berenice of Egypt's promise to the gods that she would cut off her hair if they returned her husband to her safe after a great battle. Coma Berenices was named by the cartographer Gerard Mercator in the 1550s, when, like an intergalactic boundaries commissioner, he hived the constellation off from Leo. Other constellations were named after Arab and Greek mythology, and later discoverers have played pick'n'mix with history and art when naming their findings. Some are utterly prosaic, such as the Air Pump and the Pendulum Clock, the Coathanger, Jewel Box and Coalsack, but others, particularly those borrowing from Greek mythology, speak to an imaginative process that by far exceeds the things, these fanciful patternings of objects in the night sky, that they describe. Certain theological and philosophical beliefs drove medieval man to re-draw the universe in ways that pleased contemporary thought – islands, for example, were often drawn as star shapes on maps, Paxos among them, in an attempt to make nature fit in with certain religious beliefs – but not even that can explain the tendency of astronomers over the centuries to populate the firmament with dead gods, mythical heroes, strange beasts, emblematic objects, freemasonic icons, geographical features, and even mischievously mundane objects (Coathangers? Coalsacks?). Especially when these constellations bore little or no resemblance to the things that named them.

And here they are, sparkling over Paxos, patient, reliable, innocent of the interpretations we so keenly impose on them. They are in fact the things that first enabled man to start exploring and mapping his Earth. Of course, they don't really sparkle; this is due to fluctuations in the Earth's atmosphere. There are stars whose nuclear processes do fluctuate, the Cepheid variables, and binary stars circling each other, where a brighter star will eclipse a weaker star, and then vice versa, but these are rarely seen by the naked eye. When stars twinkle, it's due to weather, or pollution.

Over Lakka they produce night skies out of science-fiction films, big skies, nights full of meaning, skies to be watched for arrivals ('Watch the skies! They're coming!'), skies to peer into prior to departure into them. In Vasilatika, over the dry-stone wall, on the clifftop, you are in the cockpit of Spaceship Vasilatika. Stood beneath this vast disc of lights circling overhead, feet planted firmly on that solid rock, it is difficult to believe that through a giddying set of circles and ellipses – the Earth's rotation, the 'precessional' wobble at the northern celestial pole that takes 26,000 years to complete its cycle, the Earth's orbit around the sun, the vast eddying of the galaxy, and the motion of the galaxies around the universe – Spaceship Vasilatika is barrelling towards oblivion at millions of miles an hour.

SEVEN

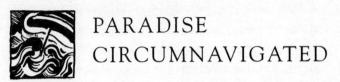

PARADISE
CIRCUMNAVIGATED

THIS SEA has had a good three or four goes at killing me.
There was the waves-coming-through-the-windows
episode of that first voyage here aboard the *Kamelia*. There
was an October morning when the *Pegasus* felt as though it
was going to turn turtle in the huge waves between Paxos
and Corfu. There was also a May afternoon, one of those
days when a calm sunny morning turns bad on you, a day
when storm clouds appeared over our destination, Anti-
Paxos, and we had to sail back round the southern tip of
Paxos and head north, into the teeth of a south-westerly
Force 6 or 7 gale. It was no fun for Graham, crouched
beneath the coaming as a friend's yacht bucked through
waves that were breaking over the bow and drenching the
skipper, Martin, and I in the open cockpit. Despite being
soaked to the skin, I was enjoying this immensely: no theme

park could match this wild and exhilarating ride. Until, that is, I mis-timed a wave while trying to shift my position, half-stood in a crouch to move, and was walloped so hard by the boat flipping up on a wave that I was almost popped over the side. My souvenir from that voyage was a bruise the size of a paddle that stretched from my left buttock down to the back of the knee.

I don't take these attempts personally, as I'm far from alone in the queasy élite of those who have found themselves in peril on the high seas. Stories of what the Ionian has done to people on or around Paxos are legion. The young holiday rep who got drunk on a day trip and couldn't swim when he fell into the sea didn't deserve to die as a result of his foolishness. I don't know if I can feel so generous towards those people who, despite being warned not to, take hired dinghies out to the treacherous west coast and then act surprised when the weather turns on them or their outboard gives up the ghost. Sat in this garden, on days when whitecaps are slapping each other about in the Steno Paxon strait, I've heard the telltale put-put of an outboard dinghy, looked over the cliff and seen a man – it's invariably a man – motoring his wife and children out into that seething mess. I've often wondered about hollering a warning down to them, but long ago decided that anyone who is stupid enough to put their loved ones at risk like that is beyond friendly advice.

Others are entirely blameless when the Ionian sneaks up on them with one of its nasty surprises. Day trips to Anti-Paxos are notorious for sudden changes in weather. Once, one blustery May afternoon, a sea taxi came roaring around from the west coast, pounding through the waves and with a tarpaulin over its entire deck. Obviously, one of the sea taxi captains had been testing his motor out in the rough weather. But as it reduced speed inside the bay its captain began to peel back the tarpaulin, and people started sitting up in the boat. This was a bona fide trip to Anti-Paxos and back that had been caught by the weather. These poor people, around twenty of them, had spent the last hour or so in almost total darkness beneath the tarpaulin, with their heads between their legs as the sea taxi slammed through waves that can carry the wallop of a car crash.

Sometimes a lone caique will be caught unawares in Vrika or Voutoumi bay on Anti-Paxos. Once or twice, they have had to stay overnight on the island, improvising shelter as best they could. The last time this happened, a few years ago, the islanders came to their rescue, offering soup and blankets and a place to sleep. An earlier crew of visitors to Anti-Paxos weren't so lucky. This was back in the early 1980s, before there were any tavernas on the island. It was late season, but still very hot. The caique had about twenty people on it, prepared, as one is on a caique trip, for a day in the sun, but not for a night in the scouring cold. The smooth sea they had sailed out into so confidently that morning began to turn bad in the early afternoon, although as is often the case no one realised until it was far too late. The caique's skipper noticed the north-westerly winds blowing the sea past the mouth of the bay, but couldn't possibly have seen the storm clouds massing over Corfu for a march south. While the conditions inside the bay remained perfect – calm, warm, sunny, with only a slight breeze to muss the hair – a storm the size of the one we sailed through was heading for Anti-Paxos and the islands to the south. By the time the skipper had seen what was happening, and had to judge whether he could get his craft and charges back through the worsening weather between Anti-Paxos and Paxos, the weather was changing fast. Before he could decide on the best action, the first squall hit them, and the weather deteriorated from there on.

Here, the story becomes a little hazy, at least according to the mythology. No one who was part of this story – the Paxiot equivalent, perhaps, of the Donner party – has felt it necessary to broadcast what went on during that storm-lashed night on Anti-Paxos. They were able to improvise shelter, and by pooling their meagre supplies and rationing them kept hunger and thirst at bay. That is all we know of the event. But enough rumour has circulated to suggest that they abandoned quite a few social niceties in order to survive their ordeal. One or two rumours, indeed, have mentioned the word 'orgy'. Those in the know fall quiet, and adopt fey looks, when the subject is broached. It is hard to tell whether this is bashfulness or wilful myth-making. Intriguingly, the skipper of the caique left the island shortly afterwards.

Such stories are the oil and vinegar of the salad that makes up the Paxos mythology. I entered it myself, albeit in a small way, the day I really did come close to losing my life to this sea.

We were on a voyage around the dark side of Anti-Paxos, the west and south coasts of the island that day trips never visit. It was a voyage that would circumnavigate the parent island and its offspring. Martin had borrowed a friend's yacht for the day, a 40-foot blue and white Hallberg-Rassy, state-of-the-art shipbuilding from Scandinavia, only six months old and worth in excess of £80,000. It had a grooved wooden deck, a spacious cockpit, and a cabin with berths off it that looked like a miniaturised luxury hotel suite, with expensive carpet on floor, walls and ceiling, hardwood shelving, a roomy galley that looked as if it was equipped for dinner parties and long periods away from port, classy plumbing, all in all the perfect floating apartment in which its bachelor owner could go gadding around the world's oceans. It smelled like the foyer of a newly-built five-star hotel. Yet its permanent and already-worn coaming suggested that its owner liked taking his floating apartment bad-weather sailing.

Leaving Lakka on a boat is always an event, not least for the effort of extricating yourself from the tangle of other yachts, caiques and the mess of lines around the moorings in the harbour. It took us a good half hour to pick our way through the cat's cradle of lines that trailed out for yards and yards from the quay.

As you motor out into the bay, the familiar cauldron of Lakka bay shifts around you much like a computerised 3-D diagram changes its shape. Familiar features, previously known in certain fixed constellations, change shape: a serrated ridge of greenery running from the col to the lighthouse turns out to be three different headlands seen sideways. The cliffs and the terrain of the promontory are almost unrecognisable from down here. The col becomes a window on a wild and alien landscape of rocks and water between the island and some rocks that are said to be the petrified remains of Ulysses's ship. The water near the edge of the bay must be 30 or 40 feet deep, but it is transparent above a sandy bottom coloured a light eggshell blue by the sunshine. It is utterly smooth apart from the wash the Hallberg-Rassy is creating. Only at the edge of the bay, where sea grass and rocks cover the seabed, and where beyond the lip of the bay the sea plunges to over 150 feet, then 300, does the water darken and, rather than revealing its depths, reflects our own image back up at us.

The Admiralty chart for this region of the Ionian says that parts of this area outside Lakka Bay are sometimes 'dry' around the Ulysses rock, that is, as well as the rocks protruding from the sea there are also submerged rocks and rocks whose tops graze and break the surface of the water. These are submerged versions of the towering sea stacks to the south on the west coast; the water around them plunges almost immediately to over 90 metres, 50 fathoms, and then swiftly on to 120 metres and more. Just over three nautical miles to the west, the water is already a mile deep. That, too, is on its way down, to a full three miles, where the great whites and sea monsters cruise.

While from inside the bay the lighthouse seems to be very close to the village, in fact three sizeable coves separate it from the hills above Lakka. These are rock and scree slopes, dotted with scrub and *maquis*, and below the Lakka Point lighthouse they lead down to the island's one sandy beach, an exposed and dangerous place for swimmers, where big waves roll in from Africa.

Beyond the lighthouse the cliffs rear up in that terrifying verticality, falling into the sea like curtains, the two elements of rock and water joined at near-perfect right angles. Even on calm days, the waters beneath these cliffs bulge and subside with the swell, often long and nauseating, 'noise', as James Hamilton-Paterson's meteorologists call it, pulsing away from bad weather elsewhere. Approaching the sea caves, or manoeuvring between the cliffs and the sea stacks, despite the power of the engine you still feel that if Poseidon so wished, one of these waves could pick you up and spill you against the rock.

There are fissures, or synclines, in the rock, which have allowed the sea to eat small coves into the cliffs, and the sea has eroded cave systems at the bottom of weak points in the cliffs. Some of these geological faults, including, famously, or at least as famous as a card from Paxos can be, one that looks like two parted buttocks, also provided the sort of terrain from which the islanders carved their steps down to the caves where they hid from invaders. Somewhere up above us, as the Ipapanti Katergo rock comes into view, jutting up like a submarine surfacing at speed, is Vasilatika, as hidden now as it has been for more than 500 years. The same number of feet above us, Pano is at work in his olive groves, or rebuilding his family home.

The real stars of this coastline are the cliffs at Erimitis, an ocean-going version of Ayers Rock. On most summer evenings, and many a winter evening, too, when the sun sets with little cloud around, the sunlight makes these majestic towers of rock turn from dusty white to a deep roseate pink, then brown and black as the sun disappears from view altogether. There is a small private vineyard near the St Apostoli church overlooking the Erimitis cliffs where an island viniculturist has found what has to be the ultimate spot for a sundowner aperitif or cocktail in the Ionian, perhaps the whole of Greece. His vineyards face across a 500-foot deep chasm towards the Erimitis cliffs, and reach almost to the edge of the cliffs on this side. Into the low stone wall around his property, perilously close to the cliff edge at one point, he has inserted two pieces of driftwood, one in the shape of a comfortable chair, the other the shape of a small occasional table. We tried his chair once, a hair-raising experience for those not used to such heights, while waiting for the cliffs to switch on for their free daily show. Apparently, the vineyard owner would bring a small bottle of brandy and a glass whenever he came to the vineyard to work. I would never have believed that an after-work drink could bring such balm to the soul. However tough a day's work here is, a glass or two of Metaxa in a chair with an exclusive view of the sunset over the Erimitis cliffs could persuade someone that they had fetched up in paradise.

Apart from the sea caves, which are dramatic, particularly just before Erimitis, where one cave system is flooded with sunlight falling through a hole on the ceiling caused by a rock fall, and the one that the mythology insists housed the famous Allied submarine during the Second World War, the west coast begins to subside from here. Past Prasses bay and Mouzmouli, where there is a sheltered beach, just below but inaccessible from the southern village of Vellianitatika, the land gives out to grass and *maquis* that probably haven't been worked for decades, perhaps centuries. Curiously, however, this land, right down to the channel that lies between Paxos and the notional island of Moggonissi (now linked by a causeway), the hillsides are neatly divided by tidy drystone walls, suggesting either cultivation or grazing, or a portioning out of ownership of the land in the past. Just before the mouth of the Moggonissi channel, this vegetation peters out entirely, giving way to stark fields of worn and pitted limestone, nubbly like molars and tufted with tenacious lichens. The last lump of Paxos, the tiny islet of Kalchionissi, looks like the sort of blasted rock that William Golding's Pincher Martin washed up on.

A mile or so away, Anti-Paxos looks nice enough to eat. Here, the islomane theories of Durrell and Hamilton-Paterson really do start ringing bells. It looks so small you could pick it up. If no one was looking, you might even slip it in your pocket and take it home with you. Certainly, you could imagine living there all on your own, perhaps with a couple of velociraptors to scare off the day trippers, and given the arms you could definitely defend it against landing parties. Even with the day trippers, as soon as the sun began to sink in the west, the trippers would flee the shadowing beaches of the east coast and head off back to Paxos, leaving you to savour the twilight on Anti-Paxos as God started inking in the air between the trees, the sea between the two islands, and the sky above them. Time, perhaps, to put some Ellington or Satie on the CD, slosh out a few fat gin and tonics, and start tinkering in the kitchen. After dinner, you could wander out into the garden or terrace, gawping at the Milky Way, and like the people on the cliffs at the top of Paxos, complain about the skyglow produced by the vulgar distractions of the towns on the island just to the north. No disco or metal or *syrtaki* would leak as far as Anti-Paxos. The only night sounds would be totally ambient: just you, the cicadas, the murmuring Ionian, the weather, and the velociraptors crashing through the undergrowth.

Most vessels approaching Anti-Paxos head for its heart; the beaches of Vrika and Voutoumi, site of at least one afternoon of satori for your correspondent. These beaches are said to be among the best in Greece, offering swimming and snorkelling that rival the Caribbean, although these factoids recur in so many holiday brochures that they are probably clichés which grow with their own repetition and now have a life of their own. The beauty of Anti-Paxos is in fact its water's distance from any source of pollution; a water so clear, so blue, so beautiful, so inviting, that it can induce a modern-day form of calenture, or sea-madness, in the visitor. Centuries ago, when British exploration of the world's oceans was at its peak, calenture was described as a fever induced by the heat of the tropics, possibly around the doldrums, which would lend an interesting meteorological slant to Samuel Taylor Coleridge's 'Rime of the Ancient Mariner'. Seamen suffering from calenture would imagine that the sea was in fact lush green pasture and be overcome by the urge to jump overboard and gambol in those green fields. The notion was so common that it recurs through the seafaring literature of the period. It is mentioned by Raleigh, Defoe and Swift, the last of whom committed the condition to (rather hobbled) verse: 'So, by a calenture misled,/ The mariner with rapture sees,/ On the smooth ocean's bed,/ Enamell'd fields and verdant trees.'

The *Complete Oxford English Dictionary* gives calenture a variety of meanings beyond the medical condition afflicting men sent mad by months and even years detained, often against their will, on small craft forging their way around the mysterious globe. It has a root in ancient French, as well as Spanish and classical Latin, and each variation – Calenture, Calentura, Calentar, Calent-em – refers to heat, burning and fever. Its Spanish variant overlaps with sunstroke. Defoe's Crusoe 'was continually sick, being thrown into a violent calenture by the excessive heat'. Calenture also took on medical and moral overtones, of sickness, mental derangement, and base passions. Andrew Marvell, he of the famed line, 'Come live with me and be my love', appropriated it as a metaphor of thirst or ambition, and more commonly it was also used to imply 'burning passion, ardour, zeal, heat, glow'.

Anti-Paxos is nowhere near the doldrums or the tropics, but I and untold others have known calenture there, staring down at the light blue jelly that separates us from the smooth sandy seabed twenty or thirty feet below, gripped by an urge more violent than vertigo, the overwhelming desire to throw ourselves into this other medium, rupture that undulating plane where water and air fizz and repel each other on the subatomic level, to succumb and surrender to the coolness and wetness of immersion, becoming animal again, becoming fish, opening our eyes on a new planet, responding to conditions in this inverted world with reflexes lost somewhere in our DNA. The only other time we have experienced this was in the lulling amniotic fluids of the womb. The notion that this is a pleasurable experience – would we feel the same about immersing ourselves in any other medium, say, walking into a room full of gas? – is so profound that most of us take it for granted. Others are only too aware of this deep-seated *nostalgie de la deluge*. The water and immersion imagery of certain forms of advertising – drinks, cleansing agents, cigarettes, fashions, perfumes – all speak to this prehistoric memory in each of us.

Nowadays, calenture would be identified as a stress-related syndrome affecting people whose work keeps them at sea in a confined environment for long periods of time. It would probably be treated with therapy and counselling, instruction in stress-reduction techniques, and perhaps negotiations with the employers about the length of time workers spend offshore.

Back when calenture first became known to men, when they were heaving around the globe on something smaller than the *Kamelia* and relying on the wind for energy, they just had to tie the leapers to their bunks until they cleared the doldrums or until the weather turned. It's possible that they let some throw themselves to the sharks. Nowadays, on – well, in fact, off – Anti-Paxos, the water inspires a safer form of calenture, the urge to throw yourself at that transparent ultramarine silk rippling beneath the yacht, cleaving that beautiful turquoise sheen, risking only the rare, accidental brush with a small purple jellyfish that stings like a bumblebee.

Down here beneath the waters around Anti-Paxos, soaring back up towards the dancing white line of the surface, it sometimes seems that Anti-Paxos may have been thrust up out of the sea to prove an eerie paradox about boats; the fact that, after their primary function of getting you from A to B, for work or pleasure, and for living in while doing these things or inbetween doing these things, their next most important function is as a platform for throwing yourself into the sea. Wherever yachts and similar craft moor in warm waters, at least where there isn't a real threat of sharks, you will see them doing it, nutters headbutting the ocean, divers dreaming of a prehistoric time when they swam with dolphins.

We were no exception, although this particular morning we were on a different trajectory, one that would take us around Anti-Paxos before we could moor and take the plunge. Crossing the mile-wide strait between the islands, we veered to the west, catching tantalising glimpses of the waters in Vrika bay as we headed for the side of Anti-Paxos that few tourists see.

The terrain of Anti-Paxos's west coast is similar to that around Lakka; a layer of worn limestone skirting the island like a plateau about ten feet above the sea level. The island is much flatter than its sibling; its highest point can be barely 100 feet above sea level. There are few olive trees here. Most of the cultivated land is dedicated to growing the grapes for the Anti-Paxos wine.

This north/north-west coast is virtually deserted, apart from a few small houses half-hidden in the bushes and trees. Very few of the houses have jetties or means of approach visible from the sea, and it's quite possible that the islanders, and the few brave tourists who have begun renting property here, may have to use the same beaches as the day trippers do to come ashore.

Beyond the cliffs of Akri Katouvrika, the northernmost point of the island, the terrain and seascape become almost wholly alien. Paxos has shifted round on its axis to become an unrecognisable landmass across the sea. As the unfamiliar landscape drifts by on the port side, so new islands and submerged reefs loom from beneath the water. I was posted at the prow on lookout for rocks and reefs, but had difficulty communicating with Martin in the cockpit. This, I realise with hindsight, was an omen of things to come.

As the yacht passed the Anti-Paxos lighthouse – a lighthouse now automated, although only recently; a colleague once surprised me with the declaration that she had recently been befriended by its lighthousekeeper – the change in landscape was dramatic. The purply-brown mountains of the mainland rose magnificent in the east, and Paxos to the north-west now presented itself as a narrow hump with dramatically carved sides; imagine, perhaps, an elephant known solely by its side view suddenly being spied in end elevation. Motoring out into this view, barefoot on the sun-warmed wooden deck, hanging on to a stay as the yacht nosed into a light breeze, surrounded by unfamiliar sights, produced a sense of elation, and freedom, however illusory. In one of the epiphanies that happen quite frequently around these two islands, it seemed that we could be anywhere in the world, doing anything, or nothing, the Bounty ad without an end.

We moored in Voutoumi bay, and Martin and I rowed ashore for a bottle of wine and a few beers for a frugal lunch on board. The calenture got in the way of lunch, and I had to go over the side from the pulpit rail at the prow, perhaps ten feet above that sublime rippling blue, enough to make submersion, flight and surfacing a plunging submarine rollercoaster ride. The light below the blue water is extraordinary, and might compare with the ectoplasmic glow that some people feel themselves drawn towards in near-death experiences. I can't swim properly, but am confident enough to know I can stay afloat and move around, fitfully, with a lazy backstroke or a particularly pathetic breast-stroke, which is enough to get me back to where I started. Swimming to get places, or as a competitive sport, seems to me as mad as running for the same reasons. Swimming is a thrill thing, running a means of escape, or, at worst, a means of not being late for an important event. The diver captures the power of flight, however fleetingly, even if it ends in the manner of Icarus. It's a more naturalistic version of the split seconds of weightlessness one feels on certain rollercoaster rides, a thrill I have pursued from Coney Island to the Prater funfair in Vienna, and without all that machinery, com-merce and company. It's just you, a boat, the intervening air, and water. For a second or two, you acquire the air-sea skills of the cormorant, the pelican and the heron.

All too soon we were heading out of the bay and pointed at Paxos. The south-east coast of the island is, I have to confess, dull. Parts resemble the Essex or Suffolk coastline dressed with subtropical flora and architecture from the sub-urbs of Athens. Only after you have skulked past the entrance to Gaios harbour, its seafront looking ancient and Middle Eastern in its jumble of low brown stone buildings, does Paxos begin to pick up again with swooping treelines, deserted coves and bays, the deep forest darkness in among the olives, solitary houses stranded up among the trees, tiny Loggos with its crumbling olive factory that looks like some-thing out of a death camp, and the hills bowling up around the shoulders of Lakka.

We motored on past the entrance to Lakka bay, out to sea in an attempt to catch the rising afternoon wind for a spot of sailing. Perhaps a mile or so towards Corfu, Martin gybed to catch a wind from the north-east, one that made the yacht heel over to the port side to the extent that things were beginning to slide around on deck and in the cabin. We wedged ourselves against the fixtures as Martin performed his favourite trick of sailing into Lakka bay under full sail and arriving at speed in the centre of the bay, where the wind drops away from the sails completely. This impresses the seen-it-all barflies on the quayside, especially when a yacht that is heeled over hard zooms into the bay whereas most yachts motor in slowly. The trick is to be going so fast as you enter the bay that you can afford to lose the wind behind the western promontory and catch it again through the col, which should give you enough wind power to carry you into the centre of the bay. We helped reef in the sails and began slinging fenders over the side and tying them with knots that probably wouldn't have won us Boy Scout knot badges.

Of the five of us aboard with Martin, I was the only person nimble enough to help with the mooring, and I freely confess I'm little more than an armchair sailor. We had taken the Halberg-Rassy from a mooring behind Martin's own yacht, a 28-foot Camper and Nicholson called the *Hamara*, which was itself nestling behind various caiques lined up against the quay out around the harbour, the furthest land-mooring from the village. Martin asked me to jump from the prow of the Hallberg-Rassy on to the stern of the *Hamara* to take a line across it on to shore. Standing at the prow, holding tight to two stays, I waited for the signal as we motored up towards Martin's yacht. At one point, Martin asked if I was ready to jump. I mis-heard this as an order to jump – and we were closing in on his yacht fast – and I made ready to jump.

What happened next seemed to happen in a sort of dream time. I can remember everything that happened, although I don't know how reliable subjective memory is in such an event. The actual jump, or fall, isn't in the memory. I was on the pulpit rail, and then I was falling, dropping past the *Hamara*'s stern, having failed to gain a foothold, arms out instinctively to shield myself, knocked back by the gunwales and then the wooden rudder, and by the time I hit the water I knew I was in serious trouble.

It happened in seconds but seemed to last a very long time, a trick of perception, maybe, as the brain stores each event, each memory, each aspect of the accident, separately, giving it narrative weight, narrative length. I was totally lucid throughout, and the memory after the departure from the pulpit rail remains quite vivid. I guess I was already in shock when I went under, and given the injuries that were later discovered I can only presume that my brain was already pumping out endorphins to block the pain messages arriving there from various parts of my body. It struck me later that this experience was very similar to the only other life-threatening accident I have had, when I was knocked down by a speeding motorbike at the age of eight or nine. Then, after a head-on impact with the bike, which threw me on to a grass verge outside our house, I remained awake throughout, and still remember my father lifting me and taking me indoors, the crowd outside the gate, him carrying me back out to the ambulance, the wailing journey through country lanes towards the hospital, the strawberry-drink look of the blood, the stitching of head, face and limbs, the clean starchy bedlinen.

I hit the sea with that familiar explosive report you hear in the ears when you jump into or land clumsily in water, followed by the hiss and roar of the cloud of air bubbles round you as you sink. I was going under the Hallberg-Rassy, which was still moving forwards, and I remember seeing the

yacht's propeller whirring at the stern. Images of boats passing overhead in movies, from *Above Us the Waves* to *Jaws*,
flashed in my mind, and I knew I had to get away from the
propeller. Surfacing, I swam away from the moving yacht,
an act which possibly saved me from nastier, perhaps even
fatal, injury, but which no doubt exacerbated the injuries I
had already suffered. I swam to a nearby yacht and hung on
to its inflatable tender, and soon a friend of Martin's who
had been on the quay clambered over and down into the
tender and held on to me. (In the way that accidents can
happen, I never got to thank him. Wherever you are,
thanks!) As I hung there in the water, I pissed myself invol-
untarily, and began to wonder if I was cut anywhere and if
the mucky water would infect me. I was in fact bleeding
quite seriously from a graze that ran from near my left
armpit to the elbow, but I only discovered that when I was
on dry land. All thoughts of sharks were, thankfully, absent
from my mind during this. It's quite possible that my mind
was censoring itself, that the shark paranoia was clamouring
to be allowed out into my forebrain, but my subconscious
was keeping this out, blocking synapses like moats to keep
it at bay. If anything had been in the bay I was trailing
enough blood into it to signify breakfast in shark semiotics.
I was beginning to notice a bruised pain rising on my left
cheek, where my arm had been pushed against my face by
the rudder, and glancing around me I noticed that the ring
finger of my right hand was pointing towards my thumb.
Dumbly, I told my rescuer in what I hoped was a calm,
apologetic voice, 'I think I may have hurt my finger.'

A south London casualty department later identified
rather a lot more than a hurt finger, but for the time being I
was in blissful ignorance and glad to be alive. As I realised
later, had I fallen in a different way, if my arms had been

pulled back by the stays on the Halberg-Rassy, I could have had my head ripped off by the gunwales of the Camper and Nicholson (although I could quip later that at least I fell off one upmarket boat on to another). Other friends arrived and helped to get me out of the water, washing the graze with bottled water and taking me to a friend's house in the village. Julie, a fully trained nurse who runs a snack bar in the village with her Greek partner, Pano, checked me out and said exactly the sort of things someone needs to hear after an accident, and someone phoned for Doctor Costas, one of the island's two doctors. I was given a small brandy, and then tea, and divested myself of all my wet clothes bar the trunks and put on a dry pair of plimsolls. Topless and soggy, I greeted Doctor Costas, curly haired, moustachioed and suntanned. Doctor Costas looked like the most handsome man on earth, and proceeded to have safe sex with me. This involved some rough stuff – 'be brave,' he cautioned, yanking my finger back into its socket and strapping it into a splint – and then, checking for nerve damage, he ran his fingertips over my torso and arms, twice, while I strove with superhuman effort to feign disinterest in this ecstatic digital attention.

Doctor Costas could find no other physical injury, and the safe sex seemed to convince him that my limbs and torso hadn't sustained the nerve injury that would be consistent with more serious damage. This early in the recovery, he was, understandably, unable to detect the broken arm, ribs and fingers that National Health X-ray machines promptly discovered in London. He advised me that I had little more than severe bruising of the upper left arm, advice that made a nightmarish journey home two days later just bearable, and suggested the maximum dosage of commercial painkillers. He then explained that he had to charge the drachma equivalent of £25 for this emergency call-out, which at the time I thought was money well spent, although (and this is perhaps a measure of the shock I was in) in subsequent encounters with Doctor Costas, who still inquires about my finger and my arm, he didn't look like the Adonis he resembled the day the Ionian nearly got me. It remains, however, my first and so far only experience of foreplay with a Greek person.

I subsequently discovered that as many as ninety-five per cent of sailing accidents happen between ship and shore, and that the accident had added my name and number to that statistic. It was nearly two months before I was fully operational again, and for the first month or so I had to cope with the quotidian world armed with just one thumb and two fingers. The left arm was in a neck and brace, and after a couple of operations the right hand had a minimalist glove puppet – Sooty dressed for an amateur Samuel Beckett production, perhaps – parked on it for over a month. These encumbrances invited complete strangers, male and female, to barge and shoulder me in the streets where I live, which gave me a terrifying idea of what life can be like for the permanently disabled and the elderly. If I'd been armed with a gun when I had the brace and Sooty on my arm, I would be writing this from jail.

For the first few weeks, I shovelled baby food, mush and adult stuff that Graham chopped up for me, with a spoon controlled by the available thumb, index and middle finger. Bathtime took anything up to an hour, keeping the broken arm out of the water, encasing Sooty in a plastic food bag sealed with a broken wristwatch to keep dry a metal bolt that had been inserted in a sliding spiral fracture in the ring finger. I had to dump old curtains into the end of the bath so that I had something to sit on and stand up from, otherwise I wouldn't have been able to get out of the bath, and on more than one occasion I sat in a bath that I had been able to drain by yanking the plug with my foot contemplating the possibility that I wouldn't be able to get out of it until Graham got home and helped me. It was weeks before I could wash under my armpits, over a month before I could handle soap. My baths could have won an Arts Council grant and rave reviews at the ICA. I learned to dress lying flat on the floor, treated the house like a minefield, and found it was more than a week before I had the strength to open the front door. I learned to be glad to be alive.

Nearly a year later, it's rare that a day goes by without the explosion and the fizz and the propeller swimming up in the memory, usually prompted by the scarred ring finger and the mildly disfigured hand. The injury kept me from returning for much of the olive harvest, but the island and its waters, and the craft that traverse them, still hold no terrors for me. I returned as soon as I could that autumn, and sailed from Lakka again the following spring, just after a magnificent Greek Easter. But it has taught me to negotiate the world with care and suspicion. This crippled hand, and it isn't really that crippled at all, is my equivalent of the Ancient Mariner's albatross. You, perhaps, might be the wedding guest.

EIGHT

ANIMALS

WHEN WE DORMICE CREEP AWAY into the hills at night, the creatures come out to play. Our reasons for leaving the village early are pragmatic: we prefer to eat early, from a mixture of habit and diet, and each glass of alcohol consumed in the village at night takes us, and anyone else with a perilous journey out of the village to their home, a step closer to disaster. People have broken wrists and ankles on the goat path (infamously, someone once stepped into the bushes on the headland for a pee and was found dead on the rocks the following morning), and I have twisted both ankles returning to this garden in a party mood. The second time was my own fault, but the first time a taverna owner insisted we toast him for his 'birthday', wondering, we were later told by informants who shall remain nameless, what

· 97

would happen on the path if he got us drunk. After two buckets of Metaxa apiece we abandoned protocols and begged off the 'birthday party'. At some point in the countless twists and turns up through the trees, my feet took a hike east when I was heading west. I ended up on my back in some bushes, my torch scything the night sky like the spotlights at a movie premiere. I was marooned up here for three days, until the melon-sized swelling of my left ankle subsided. Graham became nurse, cook, bar steward, and, this being at a time when a restaurant in the village had a genuine pizza oven and a genuine Italian cook, pizza delivery boy.

There are other reasons for leaving the village early apart from diet and road safety. Gaining a vantage point on the path above the village, turning to look back on that heartbreaking vision of stone, lights and water, one can hear the hubbub among the funlovers back in the village. One bar will be playing the Rolling Stones, another, Prince. The older restaurants will be competing with each others' tapes of *syrtaki* and maybe even *rembetika*, the Greek equivalent of the blues. Serano's, a favourite with the guest workers, some of whom park their favourite tapes behind the bar, will be pulsating with the rave beats of the Beloved, KLF or classic New Order. Harbour Lights will be full of Greeks and English shouting at each other while the windows rattle to Guns 'N Roses. In the still eye of the storm, Edward Kennedy Plaza, a tiny alley named after the senator following a brief visit to the village in the 1960s (when Jackie O was seen in the village, behind a scarf and dark glasses, accompanied by husband Ari, who was looking for an island to buy), three bars will be competing for the silence; one will be leaking Duke Ellington and Dexter Gordon, another Enya or Paul Simon, and a third, if Luciano still has my tape, The Durutti Column. One night late in this olive season, I actually heard Enya's *Shepherd Moons* leaking first from one bar, and then another, in a bizarre call-and-response that went from one side of the plaza to the other and back again.

Elsewhere in the village, the party of 40 flotilla sailors sat at one huge long table outside the Dionysos Grill will have passed the point of caring, that unsafe harbour where dignity and common sense slip their moorings. Long-forgotten party pieces, Elvis impersonations, 'Summer is Ycumen In', Beatles medleys and rugby songs will ring in the air above these sozzled choirs. And there is always, always, some old sea salt fresh from a voyage around the world who is only too happy to fetch his accordion from a boat named after a Grateful Dead album. Scarpering up the path on nights like these – and this is a factual report of the night of Sunday 15 May 1994 in Lakka, although the boat's name is a gratuitous embellishment – one begins to feel a bit like Lot's wife.

I don't recall if Lot's wife looked back on Sodom out of envy or astonishment, but if she were coming up this path behind us, her main feeling would probably be relief. In Britain, nine o'clock at night is the time when television stations can show adult material. On Paxos, nine o'clock is the time when the party animals start their rounds. This might be painting a rather hellish picture of Paxos at night – for the same will be going on in Gaios and Loggos – but the above musical portrait of Lakka on one May evening is an aerial view in the manner of John Dos Passos's camera eye. Down among the alleys, tiny squares and fanciful 'plazas', the music, noise and hilarity are actually contained quite successfully by the walls of this closely packed village. The same cannot be said of its visitors, but Lakka, like Paxos, treats them as an affectionate parent will treat a hyperactive child. (There are bone-hard economics behind this affection, but both sides conspire to ignore this.)

Paxos at night, and Lakka in particular, for this is the funkiest of the three villages on the island, sometimes comes to resemble a party scene from a musical by Bertolt Brecht and Kurt Weill. The party scene has its Pirate Jennies and Mackie Messers, its Surabaya Johnnies, its women and men looking for the next whisky bar (no, don't ask them why). Except these are called Rosalind, or Steve, or Julie, or Forbes. These are people who spend all night carousing on the beach (Rosalind), or spend all night carousing with old friends in Serano's and almost miss the ferry home (Julie). These are people who arrive, dump their bags, go out partying and are found asleep with a smile on their face on the ferry jetty the following morning (Forbes), or lovable rogues, the sort who would stand you a drink at Bill's Beer Hall in Bilbao, who disappear off on fantastical and dubious adventures and reappear unannounced in the garden four years later (Steve). And each village has its Rosalinds and Julies, its Forbeses and its Steves. They are key figures, star players, in the portable mythology that almost seems to write itself on these Paxos nights. They are part of the fabric that lures people back here year after year after year. These figures, some of them charismatic, others synonymous with scandal, spice these Paxos nights with romance and glamour, even if, in the case of two of the above, they might also wreck a bar in a brawl (clue: they weren't women). This isn't to romanticise bad behaviour – Steve and Forbes were certainly drunk, but they were also having a fundamental disagreement over serious matters which ended their friendship (so far) – simply to note that few parties end without at least a little trouble. It also has to be said that the party animals are the people who oil the tourist economy: teetotal vegetarians who boil pasta in their villa kitchens aren't going to keep Paxiots in the Gap clothes, Japanese motorbikes and new kitchen equipment they want from the tourism economy.

Each week or fortnight breeds its own mythology, its characters, its dramas. The lucky ones who spend the whole summer here, like Julie, like Steve, build up an anthology of these myths, become its custodians. Some even become the stuff of legend, if only parochial legend. I am content to stand on the sidelines, only occasionally finding myself roped in on their trips and parties. After almost twenty years of going on the road with rock groups, I can't even keep up with the Lakka hardcore when they are on a roll.

Whatever the circumstances, however, I would always, always, throw my lot in with the Lakka fun beasts than the alternative, the waspish enclave of Little Englanders at the other end of the island, the suburbs of Gaios. If Lakka late at night begins to resemble the city of Mahagonny, the suburbs of Gaios at any time of the day often resemble another fictional locale, the Sussex village of Tilling, the setting for E. F. Benson's Mapp and Lucia novels. It too has its mythology, as might be deduced from the nicknames that circulate furtively among its parishioners: The Duchess, La Contessa, Newt the Fruit and Merv the Perv, although the last two might be more Chaucer than Benson. (I once had a walk-on part in this mythology, and was nicknamed, perhaps tellingly, The Butler.) There are in fact far too many likely candidates if one wanted to identify Elizabeth Mapp and Lucia figures in this miniature Home Counties sur Mer. It would take an anthropologist of the calibre of Claude Levi-Strauss to catalogue and decode their social rituals. And it would take a mind like Roland Barthes to map their starry firmament of snobberies.

The Little Englanders have been here for around thirty years, although there has been an English presence here since the last century, when Britain ruled the Ionian archipelago, from 1814 to 1864. Because Gaios was the earliest developed village on the island, it's the place where the expatriate community first began to establish itself.

Its members are like all British expatriates abroad, at once both hypercritical of their homeland, which, because they tend to be right-wing, they believe is going to hell in a handbasket swung by lefties and progressive teachers, despite fifteen years of Conservative government, and also fiercely patriotic, entertaining romantic fantasies about a Britain that really only ever existed in films made by Ealing Studios.

You don't need to be an anthropologist to observe one basic and fundamental fact about the Little Englanders, the full-timers, the part-timers with property here, and the nouveau riche (or even – *cauchemar*! – the parvenus) who only holiday here and petition annually for membership of this ghastly crew. While some settlers, such as Pat in her olive groves in Makratika, come to Paxos to retire, blend in, assimilate or even disappear into the background completely, others, the Little Englanders, seek to erect a social order just like that in Britain, but with one massive exception. They invariably, repeat, invariably, figure themselves in a far greater position of social power than they might ever have achieved back in Britain. While their fellow parishioners may not take this act of self-reinvention entirely at face value, quite often they too are cultivating an image of a big fish in a small pool, and thus are forced to play along with the game.

The Little Englanders have their own distinct culture. Not for them the shorts and swimwear of the common tourist. Men wear trousers and shirts, their lady wives floral print dresses. Domestic customs are replicated from their behaviour patterns at home. They subscribe to a fluctuating code of U and Non-U, depending on who is being dished in Little England gossip at the time, and the Non-U can expect to be ruthlessly snubbed, even in public. They congregate at events like the Paxos Arts Festival, a misnomer for a short series of classical concerts by a nondescript string quartet who rarely play anything composed this century and, to the amusement of anyone with a vaguely musical ear, spend most of their concerts going excruciatingly out of tune because of the effect of the heat on their instruments. Le Haut Paxos turns out for these bunfights, squadrons of pale men and women (only Non-Us sunbathe) in cavalry twill and Laura Ashley prints, applauding music they barely comprehend except as a badge of social status. A number of rich Greeks also turn out for these affairs, and spend the time drinking and staring in utter incomprehension at the bizarre sawing and squeaking on stage. If you dropped a bomb on one of the Paxos Arts Festival concerts, you would probably return Labour councils in a good number of marginal Tory seats. More importantly, you would also make Paxos a much nicer place to visit.

The one good thing about the Little Englanders is that, by and large, they play these games in private and leave the rest of us in peace. Their disdainful sallies into the villages, a peek at the conditions in steerage after dinner at the captain's table, are blessedly few and far between. It is entirely possible that the reason they avoid outsiders is that, like a cheat or philanderer out of a short story by Somerset Maugham, they fear being caught out or exposed.

I have to confess that I rarely, if ever, come in contact with the upper classes in Britain. But if their representatives on Paxos are anything to go by, then there can be little wonder that Britain is in such a state. For a group who purport to represent a social élite, combining intelligence, know-how, leadership, diplomacy, culture, breeding, entrepreneurial skills, the Little Englanders of Paxos display more than their fair share of the human failings that people with the above skills aren't meant to display. Not even the classic cross-section of society from a disaster movie could fully explain its complement of mountebanks and charlatans. In the few times I have stumbled into their company, or heard reports of their behaviour, I have encountered more crooks, swindlers, drunks, former rent boys, closet gays (army, church and laity), adulterers, wife beaters, nymphomaniacs, cheats, liars, fantasists, frauds and dangerous maniacs than at any other time in nearly twenty years of journalism. As one seasoned observer of this scene said, 'It's a regular *Peyton Place*.'

Luckily, the people who matter, the Paxiots, see through them as through a newly-washed window, and the language barrier is usually enough for them to make their opinions felt without revealing them to this veritable ship of fools. Luckier still are the holidaymakers whose travail here rarely leads them into the realm of the Little Englanders: their very holidaymakerness puts them beyond the pail for the Little Englanders. Those of us who return learn to spot the Little Englanders and, with a little practice, find ways of avoiding them. When hiding in our hills and gardens becomes too stifling, we come down into the villages, but camouflage ourselves, often among the animal nightlife, like a fish taking refuge in the poisonous but welcoming arms of a sea anemone.

NINE

SIEGE

ONE WEEKDAY NIGHT of a busy mid-September in 1988, we tourists got an early taste of the Paxos winter. This happened up and down the Ionian, and in some places it lasted for weeks. Paxos legend dubbed it the Siege of Igoumenitsa, after the mainland port just north of Paxos which is the main port of call for ships carrying produce to Corfu and Paxos.

Most of us were forewarned, and forearmed. Stories had been circulating for weeks before, about strikes on the mainland and strikes on Corfu that were leaving tourists to fend for themselves in hotels with no staff and villages with no shops open. The stories from the mainland were worse: armed roadblocks blocking the roads out of Igoumenitsa, farmers driving tractors on to airport runways to stop aeroplanes taking off. These, it transpired, were fiction, but they gave the air a tinge of revolution, a frisson of terror.

The cause of this behaviour was, we were told, government inaction over industrial pollution that was spilling out of the factories of Ioannina and into a river that flowed into the sea near Igoumenitsa. It was beginning to affect water supplies, and was having such an effect on the coastline of eastern Corfu that the tourists were staying away in droves. In truth, Corfu probably invented its pollution problem entirely on its own, thanks to at least two decades of indiscriminate strip development along its coastline. Statistically, a tourist swimming off somewhere like Benitses or Kavos is more likely to encounter his own meal from the previous evening in turd form flushed out to sea that day than he is a slick of industrial effluent. But such logic rarely prevails among the people who invented logic.

The Siege of Igoumenitsa ran the length of the Ionian, with the exception of distant Kythera below the Mani peninsula in the south. While the massed staff of Corfu's hotel conurbations appeared to be forming their own Paris Commune, preparing to storm the Bastille in Ioannina, if not Athens, Paxos staged its own, rather scaled down version of the Siege. One day that September – I think it was a Wednesday – Paxos declared it was switching itself off for twenty-four hours. Whatever business we tourists wanted to transact with islanders that day would be suspended. We could go whistle.

The shops quickly ran out of the things you would expect them to run out of in a crisis, starting with the alcohol. People with a corner on the pasta and Pummaro tomato sauce market became, briefly, the Harry Limes of the Paxos tourism economy. Those who didn't have cooking facilities in their holiday accommodation stocked up on fruit, breakfast foods and snacks, or got invited to eat with others who did have the facilities to rustle up a meal. I made a vegetable pasta sauce with spinach tagliatelli. Travel company representatives warned people in advance, and checked to make sure no one went hungry or thirsty during the Siege. The islanders even apologised for the Siege. At least they left the power on, even though they switched off all the lights in their businesses.

Most people got through lunch okay, snacking in gardens or on the beaches. It was only when darkness fell that people began to feel the pinch. Even though they knew there would be no bars offering them *ouzo* or Metaxa, no restaurants offering them *mezes* or *moussaka* or *souvlaki*, the tourists still crept into the village to make sure, myself included. The darkened alleyways were constantly bisected by searching beams of torchlight, as we negotiated this unfamiliar territory. The village's dressings for summer – inflatables, flipflops, card racks, all the peripheral knick-knackery of the tourist trade – had been stripped from the village thoroughfares, rendering them as bare as they are at Christmas. Restaurants and bars had left their tables out, but their interiors were dark and the tables bare. Spiro Petrou's kafeneon was locked shut and had blinds down in its windows to emphasise the fact. The shopfronts to Steve's and the Aronis mini-market were barred, although the door to the mini-market was open and Spiro appeared to be inside, conducting some illicit business in the darkness. Only Kiki, the owner of the Romantica cocktail bar, dared to flout the strike rule. She had a blazing row with the mayor of Magazia, who drove into town to confront her when he heard about this act of rebellion. Kiki is a small but self-possessed woman from Lefkimi on Corfu, with no real ties to the island's gene pool, and she told him in a no-nonsense fashion that if he and his friends really wanted to stage a strike they should have done it at the peak of the tourist season, and not now, when only a few remaining tourists would be forced to cook their own dinners for one evening. She was staying open whatever he said. The mayor of Magazia drove home with his white beard bristling with rage.

Eventually, we crept back out of the village and up into the hills. I and a friend, Barbara, were staying at the Villa Collapso, inland from the bay, where if there's a sizeable rainstorm it begins to rain indoors, like the baffling scene in Andrei Tarkovsky's film *Solaris*, where someone is completely unperturbed when a cloudburst drenches their lounge. Lakka, like Loggos, like Gaios, like villages and towns up and down the Ionian, succumbed to the darkness. Not even the rudimentary street lights were on the village, robbing it of even the faint background light, Lakka's own little skyglow problem, that the village normally has at any time of the year. In fact, it was quieter than the Paxiot winter, when the shops and bars still open fairly regularly, and when Serano or the Petrou kafeneon become focuses for the village's evenings. When the tiny searchlights of the tourists' torches stopped sawing away in the alleyways and squares, Lakka fell quieter than any winter evening, quieter even than the special holidays that close even Spiro's kafeneon. All except for Kiki's cocktail bar. It was business as usual the next morning, for Paxos and the rest of the Ionian, and for the polluters of Ioannina, too, of course.

TEN

BORES

I COME TO THIS ISLAND to indulge what is perhaps the ultimate luxury, that of disinventing myself. I take off my
watch, lose my surname, pack away my socks and start to
forget my mother tongue. If the weather allows, I can also
dispense with most of the clothes I normally wear. I forget
about my bank loan and my Access debt, my career
prospects and my receding hairline, and I swim free in this
kind air, just another stranger in this sea of strangers. I will
never be able to express fully the gratitude I feel towards the
Paxiots for tolerating our presence on their island, year after
year, spring and autumn and, nowadays, winter and Easter,
too, with a nobility that the British rarely betray to their
visitors. Even if, as I sometimes suspect, the friendliness is
backed by a sound business sense, the Paxiots handle even

their most unwelcome visitors with a grace that sometimes verges on saintliness.

See me with a beer at a table outside Spiro Petrou's kafeneon and I'm just another *xeno* with a garish T-shirt and baggy shorts, even though these days the T-shirts are carrying increasingly hostile political messages, if only to frighten off the English weirdos. These are a few of the things I don't have at my table outside Spiro's kafeneon: a favourite English newspaper; a political opinion; a mortgage; a career gameplan; an investment portfolio; a view on what these Greek chappies are really up to; the solution to Britain's ailing economy; a place in a nuclear bunker in Essex when the balloon goes up, even though that doesn't include space for my lady wife; a factually unfounded opinion on what black people are doing to the fabric of English society. I have encountered all these and more outside Spiro's kafeneon, and sweet baby Jesus I wish I hadn't.

One of the most exquisite pleasures this island offers, after its olive groves and its seascapes, is the opportunity to disrobe of all the things that define our lives at home, to reverse the act of bricolage, of self-invention, and to write yourself anew. Or even, to adopt a Buddhist humility, to erase the past, torch history, just be yourself, not a badge of work, or wealth, or skill, or glamour. Just another lotus eater with a comment to offer on the view of Corfu in the distance, the heat this afternoon, the smell of the myrtle and thyme and olive trees, the warmth of that blue, blue water.

The island has seen more than its fair share of celebrities, anyway, in the past and in recent years, from Jackie O to Ivana Trump. Thanks to Peter Bull's presence from the early 1960s on, many of the names from English theatre – Olivier, Plowright, Finney, Scofield for starters, with the odd exotic creature like Tab Hunter – have been spotted here. Harold

Pinter and Antonia Fraser have visited and returned. Writers from Edward Lear to Russell Hoban have fallen in love with its olive groves. (Hoban used a Paxos olive tree as the entrance to the underworld in his novel, The *Medusa Frequency*.) These are just a few of the ones I've heard about. And when the owner of a small bar on a Greek island asks a Londoner to pass on his regards to a famous actress the Londoner will probably never meet, you know that the English social order hasn't so much been inverted as rendered meaningless. In their unspoilt, secluded, pre-lapsarian innocence, the Paxiots – irony of ironies! – know more famous people than we tourists do. And yet the tourists, like the E. F. Benson figures gossiping in the hills above Gaios, insist on playing these games of more and better and bigger and tougher.

Some arrive with relatively harmless cultural baggage, like the poor woman I once found myself queuing behind in Spiro's mini-market. Despite the broiling July heat, her husband insisted that he be fed his Sunday roast. She had rounded up most of the ingredients for her classic English roast beef, but wondered, amazingly, if Spiro could sell her the makings for Yorkshire pudding. Others have far nastier things lurking in their luggage. Meet Ethel, all five foot two of her, a bossy matron in her fifties from Rochdale. Ethel will tell you that she's been to Paxos more times than I have before you've had time to shake her hand. Ethel's husband Walter is a Freemason, a fact that she likes to bruit about Lakka. One of the first things Ethel ever told me was that she was going to be the hostess of that year's Rochdale Ladies' Freemasonic Night. Not that Ethel is a woman mason; they aren't meant to exist, although Elizabeth Windsor and Margaret Thatcher could probably tell you otherwise. The Rochdale Ladies' Freemasonic Night is a yearly event at which the wives of Rochdale's obviously thriving population of Freemasons get together, and who wouldn't want to be a fly on the wall at that bunfight! Ethel was going to wear a purple outfit and had got a friend to design the menu with colours to match her outfit. Every May, when she returns to Paxos with depressing regularity, Ethel brings presents or sweets for the children of the villagers she knows, whom she insists on referring to with Anglicised versions of their Greek names. (Pano, even years after Ethel began coming here before I did, is still, stubbornly, 'Peter' to this monster. Over a century after Britain ceded the Ionian Islands to the Greeks, Ethel is still running Paxos for Queen Victoria.) Ethel demands, and duly gets, full obeisance for this crude emotional blackmail. Every May, she and Walter take an apartment that lets them keep an eye on the comings and goings in the village, and their evening *volta* through the alleys and squares takes on the air of a regimental inspection.

Like the Bensonites of Bogdanatika, Ethel is here to play nasty games, as if she couldn't play them at home in Rochdale. I suspect, of course, that at home in Rochdale Ethel isn't such a social star as she is here in Lakka, despite her night of glamour hostessing the Rochdale Freemasonic Ladies' Night. Lakka is Ethel's own computer-buff God Game or Sim World, a virtual reality toyset where Ethel can play at being Queen of the Universe. Sadly, she is only one of many, and you can hear them calling to each other across the kafeneon and taverna tables at night. Terribly witty comments about the food. Terribly witty comments about their accommodation. Terribly witty comments about the Greek language. You could probably film this scene, for it is one which unfolds most nights here and everywhere else people like this go on holiday, dub on a nature programme voiceover chosen at random – Desmond Morris on termites, say, or baboons – and the two would fit each other like a glove. It is, of course, a truism that these games are being played out across the world in the places where the middle classes convene to consume leisure. But there are places, and Paxos is one of them, which have got a reputation over the years as places where you can get away from it all. Who decides to get away from it all and then takes it all with them in their luggage anyway? Who, furthermore, gets away from it all, only to whip it all out of their luggage and start showing it all off around the village? As the animal nightlife have their own, largely harmless, reasons for returning to the island, so I fear that another sort of visitor may have their own agenda to pursue in returning to the island so often, snatching a fortnight's or month's illusory social cachet from the jaws of a year when they are virtual nobodies in the deadly caste system that lurks behind the twitching curtains of suburban England.

There are also, of course, the grockles, the daytrippers who come on as many as half a dozen large pleasure cruisers from various resorts on Corfu, dallying in Lakka for an hour or so before setting off for the beaches of Anti-Paxos. They have been allocated their own position in the Paxos mythology, somewhere between the animal nightlife and the Albanians. They are, at least, fun to watch. Moreover, they spend money in the village, and, unlike us, they then go away.

The grockles appear as dots far out to sea at around nine thirty in the morning. They will have risen early in somewhere like Ipsos, Kavos or Benitses, had breakfast and boarded a day-trip boat bobbing gently on water as smooth as a mill pond. Depending on how the Steno Paxon strait is feeling that morning, the journey may be as smooth as a mill pond all the way, or at least until they reach the open sea beyond the west coast, where there is almost always swell, however minor. There are times, however, when those boats round the tip of Corfu and hit dancing whitecaps that make the boats resemble skittish colts frolicking in the waves. When they meet the north-westerly current, the boats start yawing port-starboard, port-starboard, through what looks like a good 90 degrees. The holidaymakers tend to crowd the gunwales, sitting on the side of the boat with their legs dangling over the edge, hanging on to the handrail around the ship. This is fine and dandy as they putter down the coast of Corfu, but I don't think Alton Towers has yet come up with a ride that can equal the effect of sailing through a choppy sea to Paxos while hanging off the side of a boat. A choppy passage across the strait almost certainly means fun and games on the west coast, and because these trips tend to be pre-paid extras on package holidays, the tourists have to go when they are booked, and mindful of their income these boats will go in almost everything bar storm weather. Watching these boats from the garden, as they pitch and heave, roll and plunge around to the west coast, you wonder why some day-trips to Anti-Paxos don't feature in Adlard Coles's bestselling collection of sailing horror stories, *Foul Weather Sailing*.

Some people have staggered off these boats in Lakka begging for a taxi back to their resort, unaware, in all that flying water and cakewalking, that they have become separated from their holiday destination by ten miles of rough sea with their name on it. The Paxos mythology also claims, rather improbably, that a young woman once entered a travel office in Lakka and enquired about trains back to Corfu town. Certainly, some have missed their boats, innocents or idiots who didn't hear the steamer's whistle or hooter. They arrive, panting and terrified, at the jetty just as their pleasure cruiser is steaming purposefully out of the mouth of the bay. If there are other day-trip craft around, they can probably chase their own boat to Anti-Paxos. If, as is sometimes the case, theirs is the only one in the bay, they will have to find their way to Gaios and wait for their boat to pull in there later in the afternoon. There have even been times, early and late on in the season, when these unhappy ducklings have been stranded on Paxos overnight, with only a pair of flipflops, swimsuit, towel and the price of a few snacks to their name. In such cases, however, one of the travel companies will take pity on them, although not before a certain amount of chastisement.

For a year or two we would play spooks to the grockles, KGB men in T-shirts and shorts listening in to their conversations from a bench by the jetty or from a strategic position outside one of the seafront bars – until, that is, it became unbearable. They would come off the boats in blinding day-glo one-piecers and swagged gold bikinis, Gloria Swanson's sunglasses from *Sunset Boulevard* and slingbacks borrowed from Lily Savage, the men in shellsuits or shorts and T-shirts, diamond-design nylon socks on under sandals or flipflops, either already tanned the colour of varnished mahogany or burned an alarming scarlet that looked like it would glow in the dark. The men, plopped into an alien environment and feeling that they had their masculine image to maintain, were immediately on the defensive, gripping shoulder bags against the possibility of mugging. Our first grockle sound bite was: 'It looks like Canvey Island!'

We almost always followed them to Basta's Bar, an outdoor café serving booze, snacks and sweet Greek desserts like *baklava* under a fern awning at the end of the quay. It usually being around eleven by the time they got to Lakka, the men would have a beer, the women tea or coffee, the kids a soft drink, and all three would probably have a sweet snack, despite the fact that there were dozens of wasps cruising in the darkness beneath Basta's awning, and despite the evidence of the glass-bowl wasp traps that hung above each table, their interiors lined with honey, which attracted the bees and wasps who, once inside the glass bowl, couldn't get out. There would invariably be at least one doomed insect thudding against the side of the glass in each trap, trying vainly to escape, its knocking surely making apparent the fact that these things were hung here because Basta's had a wasp problem.

Mum's coffee was probably the only thing the wasps weren't interested in, and even then they'd probably fly in low to have a look. Each morning of the season, it would only be a matter of time before someone – usually the male in the party – found something to start swatting at the wasps with. Mum and kid(s) would either be cheering him on or telling him to leave them alone. Sometimes, they would get up and run around inside Basta's awning, and it got difficult to tell who was chasing what and vice versa. Once or twice it even looked as though someone was re-staging the famous schoolhouse bird-attack sequence from Alfred Hitchcock's *The Birds* right there under Basta's fern awning.

By the time they left, there would be a scattering of abandoned cakes with delighted wasps crawling over them, or beers and lemonades with drowning wasps going to heaven in them. But the visitors, many of whom spent their time in Lakka with their backs to one of the most heavenly views in Greece, wouldn't leave without some comment. 'There's nothing to do,' said one. 'They need go-karts and a daytime open-air disco,' suggested another. 'What a dump,' said one woman. 'I hope Anti-Paxos's better than this,' said another. 'Let's get out of here.'

These were, at least, largely passive in their antipathy towards Lakka, towards the island and towards Greece and its Greeks. Others manifested a xenophobia that made you wonder why they went abroad in the first place. Like the Bensonites of Gaios, they considered most Greeks to be, basically, peasants, untrustworthy people to be treated like simians. Even the simplest commercial transaction could take on the air of a full-length Mike Leigh play. When trippers, confused by a language in which something like nay means yes and something a little like okay means no, start using mime and baby-talk, I want to curl up and die.

We once observed a Scotsman ordering some beers to take to the beach from a bar on the quayside. We had long ago abandoned the sport of spooking the grockles, traumatised by the things our fellow Britons could get up to or say in other people's countries. We happened to be sitting near a wealthy Paxiot businessman, a man of fastidious manners and dress, who returned to the island whenever business allowed. We were merely on polite nodding terms, but he was always gracious when he greeted us and we hoped we reciprocated.

The Scotsman appeared, blocking out the sunshine, and asked the bar owner, Stefano Apergis, who doesn't speak English (or at least doesn't let on if he does), for two beers to take to the beach. Twigging a little, Stefano reappeared with two bottles of beer and glasses, offering to open the bottles. The Scotsman rolled his eyes, as did the Greek businessman. 'No, no,' he insisted, irritably. Cans. Cans. CANS. He drew a can in the air. '*Ohki* cans,' said Stefano. By now, the businessman was doing aerobics with his eyebrows. Madly, I thought I'd offer a little help here.

'There's a shop just up this alley that's got ice cold cans of beer in its fridge,' I offered helpfully.

The Scotsman turned and glared at me as though I had just mugged his granny.

'Cans,' he repeated, turning back to Stefano Apergis. 'Beer. BEER. CANS. FOR. THE. BEACH.' He began an elaborate mime of carrying a tray to the beach, and started making swimming movements. In London, this might have won him an Arts Council grant. In Lakka, the Greek gentleman had progressed from eyebrow aerobics to shaking his head in quite frank dismay, and I was experiencing a deep-seated urge to crawl under the table.

'BEEER,' he said, slower this time, so that Stefano Apergis would understand him. 'CAAAANS. BEEEEEACH.' The Greek gentleman was bristling with indignation, and by now I was doing aerobics with my eyebrows.

The Scotsman must have thought he was so far into this little scene that there was little chance of extricating himself with dignity so he might as well brazen it out. Thinking on his feet, the Scotsman changed tack. 'OOOOPENER?' he mooed, miming opening a bottle. Despairing, and perhaps hoping to just get rid of this pest, Stefano Apergis gave him two bottles of beer and an opener from behind his counter, mimed that the Scotsman should return the opener, and walked off in disgust. Giving us a contemptuous sneer, the Scotsman trotted off to the beach, happy at this Caledonian triumph over the forces of barbarism.

'We're not all like that,' I told the Greek businessman, shrugging my shoulders apologetically. At least he allowed us a smile.

Even this pales in comparison to a phenomenon I have observed at Corfu airport. Thankfully, it doesn't appear to have reached Paxos, although I've spotted some likely culprits in places like Sivota and Parga on the mainland. Extra vigilance by certain authorities has removed the evidence, but I don't think that means the problem has gone away.

I encountered it in the form of graffiti on the walls of the men's toilet in the departure lounge at Corfu airport. It was in a thick, black, wide-gauge indelible ink marker scrawl. I still find it boggling to contemplate the sort of mind that will pack black wide-gauge indelible markers along with its suntan lotion and its swimming trunks. The graffiti said things like NF RULE and WOGS OUT and NIGGERS GO HOME. Similar sentiments were splattered around the walls, interspersed with swastikas, not all of them with the tines facing the right way, which in fact returns Hitler's swastika to the original Indian peace sign which the Nazis misappropriated.

A few vigilant souls had taken exception to this crude sloganeering and added their own editorial comments on this outpouring of moronic spleen (I have to confess I borrowed a felt-tip and added my own rejoinder). Beyond the mindboggling fact that they should take their markers on holiday with them, one wonders what territory they imagined themselves to be in that they should start insisting that people be kept 'out' of it, and that others should be sent 'home'. In the no-man's-land of an international airport lounge, where exactly is out, where in? And where, precisely, is home? Margaret Thatcher, on walkabout in south London, once collared a woman of African descent, probably hoping for some publicity on the back of the tinted folk from the Commonwealth. 'And where do you come from?' she asked, with that sweet murderer's smile of hers. 'Tooting Bec,' the woman told her.

Here, in the men's room at Corfu airport, we had found the tribal scratchings of the fabled cavemen of not-so-mythical Benitses and Kavos, the donkey-stabbers, taverna-wreckers, the much-feared party beasts whose all-night carousings along the coastal strips of the island have produced a summertime skyglow problem that beams into the sky over southern Corfu like a miniature aurora borealis.

Statistically, of course, the cavemen must have reached Paxos, by day trip, but for some reason they didn't bring their wide-gauge black indelible markers with them. I've not particularly noticed them among the crowds off the boats, whereas I have spotted them at large in places like Sivota on the mainland, and as recently as a few weeks ago: ugly, sour-faced cretins with sickly, pale and spotted skin, Union-Jack hankies tied to their heads and T-shirts announcing their preferred knockout tipple – McEwans, Tennents – over shorts that also bore the insignia of their nation's proud flag. Their surliness was probably inspired by fear of the unknown, but that's still no excuse: they're not the only ones who are scared of situations where they are not fully in control, and others have the optimism to trust in the comfort of strangers, a trust that is often handsomely rewarded in a country like Greece. Have the last few decades in Britain made them like this, or would their precursors, the greasers, rockers, Teds and skins, have behaved the same way had they been able to travel to Corfu airport men's room and Benitses in the 1950s and 1960s? Someone once wrote that the British discovered the concept of Abroad when their men went there to fight two world wars. From the men's loo at Corfu airport, you'd be forgiven for wondering if the hostilities ever really ended.

Perhaps the most important fact about all this, the Ethels and the grockles, the Scotsmen and the cavemen of Kavos, is that both islands, poor Corfu and luckier Paxos, find it in themselves to welcome these monsters – and the rest of us – with a graciousness rarely found in the British Isles, even if in the case of coastal Corfu (the cavemen rarely stray inland), the grace may be a little bedraggled, battered and bruised. As all these people know full well, such behaviour at home in Britain would lead to social ostracism, or the arrival of the police. They have realised, however, that for cultural and economic reasons, the Greeks will by and large turn a blind eye to it. When all the factors are added up, I believe we owe a great debt of thanks to the long-suffering Greeks.

And while the monsters might seem to break down along class lines, the birthplace of democracy is canny enough to notice that this problem is in fact classless, and treats it accordingly. The English working class, which I would define as unskilled and semi-skilled and skilled blue collar workers, are as likely to fall in love with the aesthetic aspects of Paxos as the upper class, which I would define as professionals and society, are likely to abuse it.

In fact, Paxos, or Lakka at least, seems to have developed an unusual mix of classes among the people who return, with a preponderance of upper middle class who are far and away the most ill-behaved of all the visitors. (This is borne out by the private opinions of islanders.) Their manners, among fellow tourists and among islanders, are often breathtakingly rude. Ironically, these are the people who arrive with hardback Proust in their pockets, or a well-thumbed copy of Vickram Seth's *A Suitable Boy*. They have fluting, culchahed accents, and carry themselves through the world as though they were the only people in it. Again, they may behave like this out of fear, but, again, that is no excuse. I have lost count of the times I, we, have been barged, elbowed, swept aside, barked at, pushed in front of and abused by these people. Over the years, I have come to the conclusion that what this island, this village, really needs, if only to remind these horrendous people that they don't own the world, is a boatload of dykes and darkies.

ELEVEN

HEATWAVE

A HUGE and more or less static high pressure system lay across Greece. Hospitals in Athens were evacuating patients to the mountains. Droughts and water emergencies were being declared across Greece. People in Athens were being asked not to drive into the city, as the Los Angelean smog that lay over the city was almost as dangerous as the spiralling temperatures. The sick and elderly were said to be dying in their hundreds from the effects of the heat. And life on Paxos might justifiably have been described as almost unbearable.

High summer on Paxos, like high summer on most Greek islands, is a strange and for many intolerable time. The weather which for some people typifies Greece and the reasons for going there is at its peak. At times like this, the shadeless islands in the Aegean must feel as though God has put them on a slow roast. The high summer months of July and, particularly, August, are when islanders with tourist businesses will make the bulk of their money. A combination of factors – the weather, the popularity of the high season, and the fact that holiday companies and other services charge the most during this period – also means that a particular type of tourist visits Greece at this time of year: the rich, the wannabe rich and the wannabe-thought-of-as-rich. In an alliance not so much unholy as infernal, islanders have to get into bed with these people to make their money. Greek restaurateurs and other business owners, mainly affable people trying to turn an honest buck, need these monsters as much as the monsters need them. On Paxos, high summer is when Greeks in the tourist racket let their work take them to the brink of physical and mental breakdown while the tourists play gladiatorial games of one-upmanship among themselves. The three villages of Lakka, Loggos and Gaios begin to display all the worst aspects of every large social event you can imagine. Henley with hand guns, or Ascot with flick-knives, might be a good starter. And that's just the English.

Paxos might as well plant a FULL UP sign bobbing in the Steno Paxon strait during late July and the whole of August. Pity the poor islandhopper who gets off a ferry in Gaios or Lakka expecting the swarms of little old ladies in black plucking at their sleeves who they have encountered on other islands. What accommodation that hasn't been pre-booked by the travel companies, sailing schools and independent local accommodation agencies has probably been taken by the droves of wealthy Italians who inundate the island during the high season. High season on Paxos is a time of often extraordinary phenomena: some tavernas are

· 123

taken over by extended Italian families, others develop lengthy queues for tables, some even start taking bookings for tables, and still others will make you wait two hours to be served. It seems a foregone conclusion that whatever arrives on your table, whenever it arrives, will not have had the customary modicum of culinary skills lavished on it. The cook's either drunk or in a rage, the help are a few heartbeats away from cardiac arrest and the couple at the next table got served half an hour before you did. You also forgot to notice the long line of tables just behind you, which is about to seat perhaps thirty or forty people from an English flotilla sailing holiday. They are young Home County Conservative voters who think that wearing admirals' caps and shouting at each other down the length of the table is incredibly humorous. Before you have managed to finish your meal and flee, some of them will start throwing food.

In temperatures hovering just below 100 degrees, this can make Paxos seem like hell on earth rather than the heaven most believe it to be. Daytime temperatures make spending any length of time in the sun, regardless of the highest factor sunblock, dangerous, and not just from the long-term threat of skin cancer: heat exhaustion and sunstroke are things that can creep up on you unexpectedly, aided by alcohol, diet, history of illness. There is a story of a middle-aged man sitting on the main beach in Lakka one stifling hot summer day, who sat oiling himself for an after-lunch sunbathe, told his wife he was going to have a lie down, did so and never woke up again.

The sun during a heatwave is so strong, so unrelenting, like the heat that made the Thames boil in *The Day the Earth Caught Fire*, that the island can disappear in the glare. When we went for a quick spin to the west coast one morning in a friend's rented speedboat during this heatwave, swimming ashore on to a tiny shingle beach guarded by limestone arches below cliffs rising 500 feet above us, the combination of sun, sea, shingle and stone produced a glare effect akin to polar white-out. We stayed long enough to dry ourselves then sped back in the blinding glare before the full heat of the day took hold. Madly, others were pottering out to sea in small powered rowboats for a day in this marine oven.

The heatwave is such, in fact, that the temperature persists well beyond the hours that the island might normally be said to be warm. Outside the high season, most people need to carry a light coat or jumper at night. Most mornings are temperate, and unless you are sitting in direct sunlight you might dress for breakfast in warm clothes that you will probably discard as the temperature increases during the morning. In this heatwave, even in rooms out of the sun that might be described as cool or even damp at other times, we wake with sweat running into our eyes at seven in the morning. Our beds are soaked in sweat. On an island where we normally live outdoors, we spend the day devising strategies to lead our lives out of the deadly glare of the sun.

One of the few things that meteorologists are willing to predict is that long stretches of the same weather will often produce further periods of similar weather, and after a week the heatwave seems to have built to such a ferocity that it is burning off any other weather that might be approaching the region. At night, we sit in the garden gasping in the airless heat, wondering when the temperature will begin to drop. Most people agree that at about nine at night, the prevailing climate and geography, particularly the surrounding sea and the prevalent north-westerly winds, will produce a breeze off the sea that should cool the land. At midnight during the heatwave, shirtless and in shorts, we still sit in the garden, going quietly mad from a temperature that is still burning the skin, feeling waves of hot wind blowing off the island into the sea, a dramatic inversion of normal weather patterns. The sensation is like sitting next to an oven that is constantly being opened and closed, producing waves of heat. Weather lore holds that the land cools more quickly at night than the sea, inviting fresh sea breezes onland. The Paxos heatwave turns that nostrum on its head with gusts from the mouth of a volcano.

A compensation of the Paxos heatwave, unnoticed because everybody takes it for granted, is that the islanders are used to this weather. They live in houses with walls two feet thick, hidden in places where direct sunshine rarely strikes, dark and sometimes musty places, which feel like ice-cool air conditioning when you step into them out of the heatwave. If the Greeks reacted to the heat in the way that their visitors do, this island could become a war zone.

The conditions are already there for a confrontation. Occupation, of accommodation, of restaurants, bars, beaches, shops, even the open air, has long since passed optimum and is headed for overload. Hence those queues for tavernas and the two-hour waits for a bowl of pasta. (This last may be incompetence, but it is also commonplace.) Paxos is sorely pressed to express its charms in times such as these. Worse, the overcrowding, the queues, and the delays in service only make the visitors all the more bullish than they were when they first arrived; these visitors, arriving with their money and attitude, being naturally bullish individuals.

This island, these villages, just weren't built for crowds like these. The public spaces in the villages begin to resemble the West End of London after an international football match with an unhappy result for the home team.

The bars and restaurants seethe with the sort of aggression most of us come to Paxos to forget, that strident posturing you encounter if you make the mistake of straying into Soho on a Saturday night. Frequently, things turn ugly. This is a season of shouting, obscenities, violence in the night. The Paxiots are either too busy to become involved or stand back and keep their counsel, appalled but no longer surprised by the behaviour of their guests.

Sometimes one is hard put to differentiate between the behaviour of the island's wealthier visitors and the denizens of that offshore realm of Paxos mythology, Benitses-qua-Kavos, the penguin colony resorts on the south-east coast of Corfu populated in summer by English lager louts. Legends abound about their behaviour: vandalism, violence, assault, riots, worse. These can indeed be terrible places, hellish stretches of English seaside, Leysdown, say, or Morecambe, transported to the Mediterranean sun, where beaches are coated with sunbathing couples, each with a boombox at their head broadcasting their choice of soundtrack from the Our Price Top 30. I have seen people sunbathing on traffic islands in these places while a steady stream of vehicles zoomed by in both directions.

Sailing past Kavos once, a woman companion expressed mock surprise that we couldn't see the beer cans flying into the air over the resort. I began to wonder how she and her compatriots would behave in an August heatwave on Paxos. She had already made an exhibition of herself at the notorious Piano Bar in Loggos, clearing part of it by 'belting' (her term) out a version of Simon and Garfunkel's 'Bridge over Troubled Water'. Anyone who 'belts' this song has a curious grasp of music in the first place. Her eagerness to sneer at the denizens of Kavos was just a little too keen, another game of U and Non-U. Wasn't clearing a piano bar with your rowdy behaviour just a gentrified version of the hooliganism in the bars and discos of Kavos? There is a Freemasonry among these old handers, the been here umpteen times brigade, which, like Groucho Marx and his clubs, I am more than happy to forego.

Sometimes, the heatwave can erupt at the most unexpected time of the year: this olive season's clement Christmas is probably part of this weather pattern. The end of the season saw an unusually fine stretch of summery weather, too. From Easter Sunday, 2 May 1994, for six weeks until the beginning of June, Paxos bathed in weather more akin to July. (This was interrupted, for a matter of days, by storms, which then relented, and the heatwave set back in again until the middle of September.) The olive crop was in, Pano's nephew, Andoni Argyros, who manages the island's olive crop, was totting up his figures for the year, people were turning their minds to other work, and visitors were crossing their fingers that this wouldn't be another 1990, when May drowned in rainstorm after rainstorm. One night in the week following Easter, there was thunder over the mainland and dark clouds over Lakka. Ominously, a few large raindrops fell on the village, real dollopers the size of your thumbnail, sending people scuttling for cover, but, as is often the case, the weather passed us by. It had bigger fish to fry in the foothills of the Pindos Mountains, and would probably soak Ioannina a few hours later. The next morning dawned clear and calm, as would the following thirty or so days into June. Sometimes, cirrus would appear over the island, suggesting a change of weather within a day or so; cirrus can be the vanguard of new weather systems up to 1,000 miles away. Twice, sea fog, in fact low cloud, massed over Corfu and drifted languidly across to furl around the hills above Lakka. At other times stratus would drift across the sea horizon, and castellated cumulus would tower up above Corfu and the mainland, once or twice turning into anvil clouds, but none of this weather reached Paxos. Geology and geography conspired to keep it bathed in sunshine for almost two solid months. No one could remember a spring-into-summer period like this one. This late-spring heatwave was a blessing for those of us outdoors on the island, and for those with little to detract them from the diet of lotus eating. But to others, like Pano and his fellow olive growers, it was further evidence to suggest that the Paxos ecosystem was slowly spiralling out of control.

TWELVE

STORMY
WEATHER

B AD WEATHER rarely intrudes on the summer visitor's time
on Paxos, and even then that is a matter of bad luck. Of
all the years we have been visiting the island, I only remember one holiday, in the spring of 1990, that was substantially
affected by rotten weather. For the first two weeks of May, it
seemed to rain every time we stepped outside. A watercolour
kit I had brought was identified as the possible jinx – every
time I got it out, rain would start pattering on the terrace –
and I was banned from using it outdoors. After two weeks of
inclement weather, we queued at Corfu airport almost as
pale as we'd queued at Gatwick.

Inexcusably bad weather tends to save its alarums for late
autumn and winter. It was this sort of weather that brought
the bulk of the olive crop down during November while I

was recuperating with my broken arm and hand in London. I have known only one exception, an early winter storm that arrived one October in 1988, perhaps with the ferocity of the 'hurricane' that blasted the south of England around that time. We had in fact missed the first 'hurricane' because we were on Paxos, although we were around for the second. This Paxos storm exceeded the drama of the 'hurricane' we caught, and took three days to subside.

I was staying at a different villa, in the hills to the south of Lakka, at the aforementioned Villa Collapso, overlooking the east coast, on a sabbatical from my job. Graham had come out for two weeks and returned to his work, and as I'd hired a (fairly decrepit) villa for the duration, other friends joined me for a free holiday and to keep me company. In the last two weeks I was joined by Barbara, and it was during this time that we had an almost holy afternoon playing dolphins on Anti-Paxos, and a series of magical deserted lunchtimes outside the ancient Souris taverna in the village square.

We dubbed it the Villa Collapso because after an evening in the village that's what Barbara and I tended to do on the terrace; play dance music on the external speakers of a Walkman, at a level that wouldn't disturb our neighbours, have a few nightcaps, and fall around to the B52s, Grace Jones or Kid Creole and the Coconuts. I also call it by other than its real name because I am still reluctant to identify it properly: the roof sprung a million leaks every time it rained, sprinkling the kitchen like the famous indoor-rain sequence from Tarkovsky's *Solaris*, running down the electrical fittings, and during one storm it actually began filling up the illuminated glass globe of a light bulb. The interior to the roof doubled as a rollerdisco rink for the large rats which scampered happily in the vines covering the house, and the rats' rollerdisco routines involved fear-

· 131

some jumps that resounded through the Villa Collapso like doodlebug strikes. Sometimes, these explosive jettes would bring us awake with a start in the middle of the night. While Barbara and I cut a rug to New Order or Talking Heads out on the terrace, some of the rats would gather in the guttering and watch, big cartoon-shaped rats with handlebar whiskers and Mickey Mouse ears, weaving around almost in rhythm, although the weaving about was really them swatting at the fat dozy wasps buzzing against outdoor globe lights just below the gutters. The rental agency in the village feigned disbelief at the sprinkler effect, and its one English-speaking worker, Colleen, who was to become our friend, explained sweetly that the 'tree squirrels' were really quite harmless. I laughed too hard to tax Colleen about that bizarre euphemism: are there any other 'squirrels' apart from 'tree' ones? To this day, I believe the Villa Collapso still has that leaky roof and its troupe of roller-skating tree squirrels.

As the warmth began to fade away from the Indian summer and the nights started to close in, the temperate weather was interrupted by the odd hiccup of thunder at night. It is usually the case in this little corner of the Azores anti-cyclone, which dominates much of the Mediterranean's weather during the summer, that the bad weather tends to cling to Corfu and the mainland, almost as though it is forcibly precipitated on the slopes of Mount Pantocrator on Corfu and the Pindos Mountains range on the mainland. One night late in October however, this weather leapt across the ten-mile barrier between Paxos, Corfu and the mainland, and made its presence felt with a crack and a boom.

The barometer, my meteorological prison guard this olive winter, had been falling steadily. I have never travelled with a barometer, but this winter I kept an eye on it as one might on a piece of dangerous machinery, checking it regularly, fearful of what sudden plunges and surges might presage. That October, barometers and weather forecasters had villagers talking about big storms. TV weather maps showed depressions building and starting to revolve in eastern Europe and pushing down from Russia. We were drinking in Spiro's kafeneon one evening when someone, perhaps Spiro himself, maybe Pano, warned us to go home.

Neither we nor the rats went outside that evening. Indeed, the storm had the effect of silencing the rats, at least for a while; later, days later, it drove them mad, drove them, in fact, into a frenzy of rollerdisco acrobatics. They were caroming off the walls and floor up there, and we began to wonder if the ceilings would hold.

The storm announced itself with a brilliant white flash of lightning that lit up the darkened olive groves beyond our windows, and was quickly followed by thunder that sounded like timber splitting. I love storms, indoors or out, but particularly indoors. Daytime storms are dramatic and noisy, and can offer a genuine excuse for abandoning work, study or chores to watch this natural wonder. Nighttime storms are even more spectacular, bringing ghastly illumination to a landscape rendered unfamiliar and terrible by its awful light, and making the darkness itself shake. There is nothing more cosy (and, perhaps, Freudian) than being curled up in a warm bed, alone or with company, while a storm rages outside.

Soon, however, it became apparent that this was no ordinary storm, no wintry flash and rumble in the purple sky over London, no summer downpour with Wagnerian sound effects that catches you out while walking in the country-side. The amount of activity in the sky over Paxos, over this whole region of the Ionian and Epirus, was extraordinary. The storm was soon ferocious; crash after crash of thunder, flashes indistinguishable from the noises they produced. In the darkened hallway of the villa, flashes threw weird stark shadows out of ajar doors, and the changes in air pressure from the flash and explosion made it seem as though someone was igniting grenades on the roof.

As midnight approached, we decided to turn in. We checked that the shutters were secure – we usually pulled them closed in our bedrooms, if only to keep out the early morning sunlight, and had taken to leaving them open but clamped against the wall in the other rooms we used – and checked that all doors and windows were secure as well. Barbara and I had bedrooms across the hall from each other, and we left a hall light on in case of possible emergencies. Within a few minutes of getting into bed, however, we had decided independently that it was going to be difficult and perhaps impossible to sleep. The storm seemed to be building to a point where it might begin to threaten the structure of the Villa Collapso.

Unless you are struck by it, lightning is harmless, and thunder, while frightening, is merely a sound wave produced by the air in the lightning channel, which heats to around 30,000 degrees Celsius, expanding at supersonic speed. The 'rumble' of thunder is, in fact, the noise of that explosive expansion as it happens at different places in the atmosphere at different distances from the hearer. The bolt of lightning is a diagram, or, indeed, the visual score of that noise as it happens in different places in the atmosphere at different distances from the hearer. On two occasions in London, I have been under thunderclaps that have made the house bounce and set off car alarms in surrounding streets. Combined with the howling wind, this noise seemed on the verge of ripping the leaky roof off the Villa Collapso. The rain was washing down out of the sky in an endless torrent, drumming on the terrace. This was weather to go mad in.

What was all the more terrifying about this storm was the fact that the Villa Collapso was in a relatively sheltered position, just below a muddy lane in a depression to the side of a valley leading down to one of the beaches on the east coast. It was surrounded by walls, which were themselves surrounded by ancient olive groves, and yet the weather was still ripping at its fabric. The wind and violent fluctuations of air pressure sucked and blew at the windows with such violence that I feared we would be sprayed with shattered glass at any moment. And yet the storm was coming from a north-westerly direction, and the Villa Collapso was in the lee of the hills above Lakka. We were only getting whatever spilled over the hills as the storm smashed into the bay.

Soon, the *Solaris* effect began to spread from the kitchen and throughout the house; mine was the room where the rain began to fill up the illuminated lightbulb, making it look like a small goldfish bowl containing a tiny neon light. We ran out of utensils for catching the rainwater, and just scattered old newspapers about the rooms, moving beds and clothes out of the way of the worst leaks. The one positive aspect of this minor meteorological apocalypse was that the weather appeared to terrify the rats into silence.

We sat in our beds in the darkness, conducting a fitful conversation across the hallway, lapsing into silence, then calling to check if the other was okay, commenting on the changing force of the weather (hoping, of course, that it was dying away), swearing a lot and cussing the forces of nature. We finally fell asleep from sheer exhaustion around three in the morning.

When we woke again, mid-morning, to weak light creeping under the shutters, and a new sound in the trees, a white noise – zzzzzz – of relentless rain, the storm appeared to have

moved south. Investigating the perimeters of our belea-
guered little kingdom for damage, but finding none beyond
the overflowing kitchenware and sodden papers and damp
bare wooden floors, we heard the occasional muffled boom
from the south. A sky the colour of porridge obscured whatever lightning might have been producing this noise. It was
raining so hard that the water didn't have time to run away,
even though the house was on a steep hillside. The terrace
and the land beyond it beneath the olive trees was under an
inch or two of water, and it ran down the windows with the
improbable force of those suspect jets of water produced by
over-ambitious effects people in movies. At least it seemed
that the worst of the storm was over, although this was far
from the case. This was just one of a succession of weather
fronts sweeping in from that storm-generating machine, the
northern Atlantic, a serrated line on an animated map at
the Meteorological Office that passed over the Villa
Collapso some time around midnight the previous evening.
Before late afternoon the storm would be 'back', and at the
time I actually credited it with the ability to turn round over
Gaios and march back up the island to give Lakka another
good slapping. This was, of course, another serrated line
sweeping in from the Atlantic, with another bucketload of
billion-year-old water to chuck at the rollerskating rats in
the roof of the Villa Collapso. (By now, we were beginning
to wonder if the rats might not be driven down from the
roof by the weather, and whether we would get off the island
at all or be found days later, chewed up like the victims in a
B-rated gnasher movie.)

You can imagine marriages ending in weather like this.
Its initial novelty soon passes, as does the appeal of watching one element do this to another. After half an hour, the
benevolent notion that this is exactly what keeps the island

green and alive through the rest of the year is outweighed by the overwhelming conviction that this fucking noise is driving you round the bend. By now, you are chain smoking, or cracking open a succession of beers. You would dearly love to take it out on someone or something, but casting open a window and hurling abusive language at several tons of hydrogen and oxygen atoms falling through the trees at an average speed of sixteen feet a second is an invitation to the guys in the white coats with the big butterfly nets to come after you. Besides, you'd probably get wet.

Eventually, I was driven out of doors, to see what the storm had done to the village, to escape a sensation of claustrophobia that was causing the muscles between my shoulders to seize up, and to replenish our dwindling supplies of alcohol. I dressed in T-shirt, shorts and hard shoes underneath a Pacamac that I hoped would limit the impact of whatever the rain had planned for me. I gingerly picked my way down the road into the village – any faster and I would have started surfing on the sort of waterlogged surface that makes cars aquaplane – and before I reached the perimeter of the village I could see the effect the rain was having on Lakka. Skulking along beneath the whiplashed tops of the cypresses, I caught the carwash effect of the rain, a maddening spray that was blowing in every direction, including up. I might as well have been naked or in a ball-gown for all the good the Pacamac was doing me. The village was under about a foot of water, and the rudimentary drains had been transformed into fountains by the pressure of the water inundating Lakka from the sea and the surrounding hills.

Most of the village stores, tavernas and homes have slots at the bottom of their door frames into which they slide two-foot-high metal or wood barriers that keep the water out of their homes and businesses. I skirted the village and took a look at the bay, which was behaving like open sea. Waves were rolling over the submerged quayside and into the village, slopping through the alleyways back into the square and the back of the village. Everything in the village bar Spiro's mini-market was closed, and Spiro's took a hop and a skip from a dry hummock of roadway to enter via a side door. Packing my rucksack with dry and wet provisions, I swam back up the hill, a salmon returning to spawn in the Villa Collapso.

As darkness fell, another serrated line swept in from the Atlantic on that computer screen at the Met Office, almost as though triggered by the sunset. The big guns opened up over Corfu, convulsions among the limbs of the olive trees and a rattling at the windows and doors announced the arrival of a rushing storm wind. The effects guys outside turned their water machines up to full blast, and the rats, having become acclimatised to these conditions, strapped on their skates again. We were in for a hell of an evening.

Pots and fresh supplies of days-old *Guardians* duly spread, we settled down on hard Greek chairs in the Collapso front room, a cruelly bare parlour with windows on three sides, trying to read while the house attempted to depart its foundations. From the tiny square window in the bathroom, which was now singing like an Aeolian harp, the cypress trees covering the valley below us were moving around in concert like an army in fatigues rehearsing a Supremes dance routine.

The house shook, rattled and groaned, as though in complaint at this treatment. We tried drowning the storm out with Prince and the Pet Shop Boys, but the sound began to distort at the levels where we could begin to distinguish the tune above the roar of the storm. Instead, we set about improving the sales figures of a Greek liquor company that produced a vile local gin that tasted of Parma violets. By this stage, we might well have injected heroin to escape this monstrous weather.

By now we were beginning to tire of cheese and dry biscuit lunches, and the inevitable pasta'n'Pummaro dinners rustled up in the one and a half battered saucepans provided in the Villa Collapso's sumptuously equipped kitchen and dining area. In extreme situations such as this, sarcasm can be a greater lifesaver than an inflatable life belt. By the third day of the storm, when Barbara and I were becoming a little cranky, checking each other for signs of impending dementia, such as talking to ourselves, multiple personality disorders, Napoleon complexes, rescue rode over the hill in the form of Don. Well, actually he walked, but he brought with him a lifesaver, his own homemade corn chowder, which we heated on the Villa Collapso's priceless antique cooker and devoured like hot liquid manna. (These were the days, alas, before I had started baking my own bread on Paxos.) That lunchtime, the storm actually abated. Don arrived dry, and went home dry, and our last few days on the island were relatively calm. The storm had punched the summer out of the air, and nights we clung to the heat that came through the window above the Souris family's grill. We were the only tourists left in the village.

The storm was still around, though, and taunted us with freakish seas the day we waited hours for the captain of the *Pegasus* to decide that the seas were calming enough for him to take his ship out of the harbour. Only a few of us braved that journey, which, in the ferry's aircraft-type seating, felt like two hours of sea-level turbulence, dodging the bigger waves and yawing wildly across the Steno Paxon strait. For the first and only time in my life, I was glad to arrive on

Corfu from Paxos.

This was a time of other firsts as well. The airport was nearly deserted when we left, an extraordinary state of affairs for the airport notorious across Europe as air travel's answer to the Black Hole of Calcutta. The only other time I have seen the airport that quiet is in deepest midwinter.

Another, more profound, first occurred between the terminal and the door of the aeroplane. The lingering Corfiot sunshine had given way to total cloud cover, although weak, with the sun behind thin cloud. The air felt as though there was a storm around. As we queued to mount the steps up to the plane, the light behind the clouds flared and then dimmed again, and thunder boomed in the direction of the mainland. The air over the runway seemed to be fizzing with electricity. The whole area around the airfield, the lagoon, the dusty Kerkyra suburbs, the hills in the distance, was bathed in a weird browny-yellow light, like a gauze, or accumulating smog. As the flashes and echoey booms increased, nearing Corfu, the sky began to darken. We were the last on the plane, and as we reached the top of the steps the storm cracked open over the airfield and we felt the first drops of warm, heavy rain on our shoulders.

The engines were complaining against the brakes within a matter of minutes, and before the storm unloaded itself on Corfu the aeroplane threw itself down the runway and lumbered up above the balconies of the holiday accommodation fringing the runway. Turbulence inside the storm clouds made it feel as though the plane was having to hurl itself up a set of steps, but as the plane levelled off into sunshine above the cloud, for once, just once, it felt right to be going home.

140

THIRTEEN

MONSTERS

T HIS GARDEN, indeed this island, is patrolled by monsters.
Dinosaurs have been stomping around here for millions of years, even if, these days, they are rarely more than
six inches long. I have come out here into the garden to
take a squint at them, and the other miraculous fauna which
infest these few *stremas* of land. The baking May weather
continues unabated, and this afternoon we are visited by a
drifting sea fog like the star of my favourite John Carpenter
film. Corfu has disappeared behind its hazy wash, and the
perimeter of the fog is chasing two yachts across the Steno
Paxon strait. It has bowled over the petrified remains of
Ulysses' boat, and is curling up into the valleys around the
coastline. This is weather I have never seen before; what
began half an hour ago as a faint haze in the air is now furl-

· 141

ing in between the cliffs, obscuring headlands, smearing the landscape, spilling down into the bay, driven by what I guess must be warm-air versions of katabatic winds. Its perimeter is passing overhead now, blowing south, a little too high to curl a wisp of hot condensation around the screen of the Apple Mac Powerbook. As it streams into the bay, the sea outside disappears and the hillsides inside it begin to steam like library footage of far-eastern jungles. As the fog's forward perimeter passes over the garden, I'm reminded of the woman disc jockey alone in her lighthouse in the John Carpenter film. Any thicker and I'd expect those spectral hands with their grappling irons and seaweed to be reaching out of the fog. This is in fact low cloud, blown down to sea level by the wind, and bodes ill for the weather, which has been extraordinarily fine for the past month. It also bodes ill for my journey to Corfu on the speedboat tomorrow morning, where I hope to surprise Graham as he leaves the airport with his luggage: 'Carry your bags, meester?' (Actually, I was wrong: an hour later the fog had retreated, like its cinematic cousin, to hug Corfu, that most meteorologically unfortunate of Greek islands.)

This news is too big for the dinosaurs, who scuttle and pose hoping that I won't see them, unaware of these rearrangements in their universe. They clearly think they own the place, which, after a few million years of uninterrupted tenancy of these rocks and hills, they might legally claim to do. They are the stars among the fantastic wildlife that a pale and hopeless townie finds as his neighbours in this garden. Yet I have to confess that even after more than a decade of treading this territory, I step into it with trepidation, although I am not as chary as the visitor who once went faint and had to sit down when he saw an adder dozing curled under some rocks in the garden. Yet it has taken me nearly a decade to learn that wasps, creatures that I used to swat at as wildly as any other terrified tourist, mean me no harm, and that the shiny black monsters which cruise through the garden making a noise like a Lancaster bomber probably want to give me a wide berth too. Like many a tourist before me, I have sprinted from taverna tables (and returned, scarlet with embarrassment) because that most stupid of insects, the mother-of-pearl scarab beetle, which Pat calls, dearly, the flying sweet, because of its resemblance to a wrapped chocolate, has decided to fly blindly into my face, its fart-like buzz giving this most harmless insect a very menacing appearance. And once, stranded on this hillside because of a twisted ankle, I wrapped myself in a blanket despite the heat because a hornet had taken a rather close look at my injured leg.

People who go on holiday to hot places often forget that they will have to contend with the wilder inhabitants of the places they visit. This year, it is spiders. Spiders loomed large, metaphorically and literally, in my childhood demonology of the things that were out to get me. They came somewhere between daddy longlegs and the neighbourhood skinheads. Spiders appear to have intelligence and purpose, the two things that scare me most about life-forms I distrust. (Sharks are another.) This year, they are all over the place. I suspect that I may have been bitten by one, from a two-pointed bite I earned after unwisely plunging my hand into some bushes in the garden while picking up a bowl that had fallen there. For a good thirty minutes I watched for all the symptoms – racing pulse, palpitations, sweats, nausea, dizziness, hallucinations, portents of impending doom – that I thought might attend a really interesting spider bite, but none came. Boringly, this bite swelled to the size of a large acne spot then faded after a few days. I stepped down the alert for funnel-web spiders in Don's garden.

Mostly, the spiders are the size of money spiders, or the tiger-striped ones children throw rocks at in privet hedges. I have even overcome my qualms about arachnids to the extent that I sometimes carry these chaps outside rather than mashing them with newspaper, imagining myself to be doing something for the ecosystem. In the ecosystem, of course, if the roles were reversed these chaps would be eating me.

It is possible to pass along a path, in the garden or on the promontory, and find yourself breaking through hundreds of newly-spun spiders' webs, sometimes mere minutes after you have passed going in the opposite direction. I have never seen so many spiders' webs as this spring. The distance the spiders can shoot their gossamer is prodigious: in human terms, it might be comparable, crudely, to me being able to stand on the edge of the garden and piss on Kavos, a not entirely unattractive proposition. The spiders are hell for early risers, who have to be the first to break through their new webs, and find themselves wreathed in gossamer, and the odd angry spider, on the way down into the village. Sitting in the garden early in the day, you can suddenly find yourself enveloped in gossamer shot at you by a spider that has decided you might be a handy anchor for that day's web. This can be particularly creepy if, as is often the case in this garden, you are only wearing shorts.

Unbeknown to them, the spiders also became mute witnesses in a burglary case this spring. I was alone in the house, working with headphones on and probably yoyoing around to the Orb, when I heard the sound of someone breaking into a house along the promontory. I snuck along the path, collecting wet spiders' webs as I went, to investi-

gate the noise they made breaking in, and probably scared
them off with my shouts of 'Yassou!' and 'Hello!' They had
smashed their way into two properties, and made off with
some electrical equipment and other domestic appliances.
They would have systematically gone through three other
properties as well, had I not inadvertently scared them off.
The fresh spiders' webs, however, proved that whoever had
done the crime had not followed the visible path out of the
village but had taken a road that could be known only to
islanders. This took the heat off the itinerant gypsy mer-
chants and Albanian refugees who, in an uncommon lapse
from philoxenia, the Greeks sometimes blame for crimes on
the island. The crime was never solved, and for a brief while
I believe even I was a suspect, but those spiders' webs were
the Paxiot equivalent of the hair that James Bond would
lick and place across a doorjamb to see if anyone opened it
in his absence.

A country-dwelling friend once passed on the sage
advice that I should never destroy spiders' webs, unless they
became too big, because spiders' webs control flies and other
airborne pests. The spiders in this garden, like much Greek
wildlife, appear to be too sluggish to effect this handy chore.
Horseflies, with their tiny needle-like bites, visit daily, and
blue flies are around most of the time. Most annoying, however, is a breed of small, black and harmless fly, probably the
most stupid thing in this garden after me, that drift in the
air like parachutists who can't control their parachute.
These things hatch in the garden, sprout wings out of a sec-
tioned carapace, rise in the air, spot me and come over to
say hello. They love cans of beer, and mugs of tea, and find
bowls of cereal too tempting for words. These insects are
nature's kamikazes, born with the sole intent of self-immo-
lation, and usually at my inconvenience. They go mad in

the vicinity of washing, which, if you are soaking white things like T-shirts, they commit suicide in and, dying, bleed on to your clothes. They absolutely adore body hair, which they love to tangle themselves in, and will never be flicked off your body by a finger if there's a chance that you might accidentally mash them instead. These witless animals drift through the garden looking stunned, as if they haven't a care for their own safety, although it is likely that nature has not equipped them with this alarm system. Yet they have antennae, which respond to the approach of a human finger, and have evolved to the level where they can sprout delicate lacy wings and protect them with the sleek black Rover bonnet of their carapace. Mother Nature must have had a hangover the day she created these idiots, although she wasn't doing too cleverly the day she invented the man who will run around a garden with a bucketful of wet T-shirts cursing the cloud of insects drifting along behind him, either.

Sweetest of all these monsters, and I know this is shameless anthropomorphism, are the geckoes, those Woody Allen figures of the animal world, so shy they cluck and sing at each other while hiding behind different bits of furniture. The village of Puerto Escondido on the Pacific coast of Oaxaca in Mexico has made this pale and near-sightless dinosaur its mascot, which suggests that the Mexican branch of the Roman Catholic church might still be learning a thing or two from its Mayan and Aztec predecessors. Geckoes like to live indoors, where they lick at flies and other insects. There are perhaps four in this house, two in each room, each with its favourite hiding place, such as a particular picture, or a wardrobe, and on warm nights they sing love songs to each other from these hiding places, unaware that we are listening. At least, I imagine these glot-

146

tal pops and squeaks from behind the furniture to be love calls, for if a lonely gecko is only complaining about the neighbours – us – then it is wasting energy that an animal its size can barely afford. They are obviously aware of our presence, even if we are sitting reading, as they sometimes come out to check on us. They commute about the room with a terrified scuttle when they think we aren't looking, although of course we usually are. The geckoes are as cute as buttons, and more fun to watch than Greek television.

The kings of this particular jungle are the dragons that race back and forth across it every few minutes, salamanders, relatives of the iguana and both of them descendants of the gigantic iguanadon, reckoned to be about thirty feet long, with a head the size of a car and a mouth the size of a car bonnet, bigger than any shark's, with the possible exception of the whale shark. A rain of meteors is believed to have done for the iguanadon, and their saurian counterparts, by plunging the world into a nuclear winter. So nowadays we have to make do with the pocket version. There is a lizard I have seen on Corfu, about two feet long, that does rear up on its powerful hind legs, like Steven Spielberg's velociraptors, and runs around looking smally terrifying, but these are the only ones I have ever seen on Paxos. As well as decorating the place, they keep the number of insects down. Nature has a use for everything in the garden. What the dragons don't snap up, the ants carry away to their subterranean kingdom. Anything left gets recycled over the cliff, like the rats which the cats sometimes kill. We hurl these in the general direction of the sailing-school students on their windsurf boards and Lasers, with a cheery yell of 'Here's one I prepared earlier!'

Where once the skies over Paxos would have been patrolled by pteranodon and pterodactyl, and later the archaeopteryx, they are now patrolled by gulls, swifts, and the unfortunate trigonia, a tiny bird that the Greeks love to shoot. They claim to eat them, but mostly it is cruel fun. They do eat blackbirds, like the Corsicans, and other birds too. One visiting bird-spotter was distressed to find a plastic bag full of dead golden orioles in his host's freezer compartment. The swifts are too fast for the gunmen. They surf on the invisible air currents that play about the cliff face, zooming up over the garden so close you can hear the whoosh of their wings and the snat! of their beaks as they snap at flies. We once mistook a flock of swifts for a cloud of large insects, so dense was their formation. They were whirling in a thermal in the bay, and we made ready to grab our lunch and flee indoors, expecting to be attacked by a swarm of ghastly flying invertebrates. When they passed overhead they were still whirling, but we were able to continue our lunch in peace. We worry about the safety of other, slower birds, like the pair of peregrine falcons who nest on the other side of the bay and can be seen turning elegant and effortless circles in the air currents above the island. The tiny Scops owl, whose eerie tocsin can be heard in the bay, only comes out at night, and is rarely seen. But others blunder into the bay, unaware that there might be a dozen Greeks with guns hiding in the hills and all of them lining up to win a fluffy toy. A large pelican flew over the garden the other day, slow and lumbering, an avian Dumbo, but was lucky that it was a weekday, when the gunmen would have been at work.

The writer Annie Dillard once reckoned that, when she lay down on the banks of her blessed Tinker Creek in Virginia, there must have been a million living things on or beneath the area of earth her body covered. I rarely lie on the ground here, except occasionally to get eye to gimlet eye with a lizard, or in a vain attempt at fooling the cats into talking to me, but I have an inkling that there is more going on in this garden than meets the eye. The day I broke my arm, I lay awake virtually all night from a mixture of shock, terror and pain, eking out the Neurofen so that I did not overdo the daily dosage. I dared not move lest the injured arm snapped or simply fell off. I lay watching a parallelogram of the stars over Paxos through the window, chiefly Orion and the Big Dipper sliding down the sky, willing the sun to come up. It was the longest I'd spent so far watching the stars, and I spent much of the time wishing that it wasn't.

Deep into the night, the garden sounded busier than Piccadilly Circus at rush hour. Scrapes and rustlings, hoots and squeaks, scuttling and jumping noises, the sounds of foraging, courting and hunting, the patrolling of boundaries and the trespassing on the territories of other animals, filled the garden with a constant noise. At one point, something quite large padded by below the window under which I lay, and I became suddenly aware and quite nervous of the fact that there was little protection between me and whatever was padding by outside. Finally, the sunlight began spilling down off the Pindos Mountains and into the Ionian, flooding across the sea to begin lighting the rocks at the edge of the bay. As the sun rose the noise died down, and the garden seemed ours again. The night creatures had scattered, unseen. But that one noisy night reminds me all the while that the garden is only really ours during the hours of daylight, and that the monsters could take the garden back again whenever they wanted to.

FOURTEEN

SHARK JOKE

Sᴜᴛᴛɪɴɢ ɪɴ Dᴏɴ's ɢᴀʀᴅᴇɴ ᴀʟᴏɴᴇ early one April evening, reading Durrell, coddling a gin and tonic, wondering if there was bad weather in the grey clouds slipping overhead to cover most of the sky, I glanced up, catching the white of a yacht's sail as it crossed the Steno Paxon straits, and happened to see a large fish arc up out of the water, hurling its full length, perhaps six feet of it, clear of the water in the mouth of the bay. I jumped on to the low wall of the garden, hoping to see it again, but this one leap – at least, the one leap I noticed – served whatever reason this fish had decided to leap out of the water for in this exact spot.

It was my fourth sighting of what I presumed this time was, as before, a dolphin, although this fish, from the instant that I glimpsed it, seemed different from the dolphins I had sighted in the past. It looked fatter, pointier, to quote the Monty Python skit about the fraudulent dinosaur expert, thin at either end and fat in the middle. It looked more like I imagined a tuna would look in its natural habitat, and tuna are said to jump when they are pursuing small fry. But this one was on its own, and tuna run in schools or shoals.

My first sighting had been early one morning, barely past eight, aboard the *Kamelia*, heading for Corfu one September morning. The surface was like glass, as it so often is, as I glanced up from my book and out to sea. Just at that moment, a sleek black fin knifed up out of the water at a 45-degree angle, accompanied us for a few seconds, and then knifed back down below the surface. As someone who hears the music from *Jaws* in Holiday Inn swimming pools, I knew instantaneously that that fin had my name on it. The famous John Williams music was already welling up. Luckily, common sense took hold of some lower part of my consciousness, and I found myself shouting 'Dolphin!' and pointing at where the fin had been. The entire top deck of the ferry turned, and the dolphin showed its back once more. It was travelling just a bit faster than the ferry, as though playing a game of overtaking (it seems reasonable to assume that something as intelligent as a dolphin would be amused by the act of speeding past something far larger than itself, mechanical, and with humans on board). It played with us for a few minutes, before disappearing and reappearing about a quarter of a mile away, where it had found a mate. They spent quite a while playing together, diving down, shooting back up and out of the water, and spinning vertically in the air, looking for all the world as though they were dancing to rock and roll.

Another time, on one of the typically clear and still early morning summer crossings to Corfu, an adult dolphin followed alongside for part of the way, diving and swerving around near the surface. But the loveliest sighting was one autumn lunchtime in this garden. It was one of perhaps hundreds of similar days in the garden: castellated cumulus out to sea, a slight offshore breeze, but strong sunshine, enough to make us seek shelter after a short time beneath the shade of the *tenta*, a cotton awning that stretches over an ancient outdoor dining table in the garden. Lunch here is a rolling picnic. We empty most of the contents of the fridge on to a tray, take it down to the table under the cloth awning, and pick around at what was left the last time we brought the tray back up from the garden. These lunches become quite poignant, because we know that soon we will be gone and it will be seven or eight months before we are back in the garden, dozing over lunch, staring out to sea.

We had just finished lunch, when again something caught my eye. A couple of adult dolphins came around the opposite headland, as though from the west coast, heading across the mouth of the bay going south. They were taking turns to leap up and perform forward somersaults completely clear of the water, crashing down into the ruffled sea to reappear some yards later, where they would again fly out of the sea, somersault forward entirely clear of the water, as though to amuse or impress their mate, and crash down into the sea again. They continued this performance across the mouth of the bay, and may indeed have been doing this beforehand, just as they probably continued doing it as they swam round the other promontory and headed south. They could neither have known nor, really, cared about the three people up on the clifftop marvelling at their game. But the sighting suggested that nature, while red in tooth and claw, can also find time for play, and magic. This sight will stay with me for ever.

Along with the acrobatic tuna, it also pointed up something that few visitors to this bay probably realise. Playing and swimming in the shallow, sandy-bottomed water near the beach, we perceive the bay as nature's swimming pool, just as we perceive the sea as a surface to be traversed, rather than what it is, the roof of a new world filled with a multitude of lifeforms. There may be some spiny urchins in the rocks, and the odd small purple jellyfish, but the main forms of life that share the bay with us are the tiny coloured fish that nibble the hair on your legs mistaking it for algae. Yet a few hundred yards out some very large fish live, and sometimes they do come in.

Mostly, they come in in nets and baskets, on boats like Akis Petrou's, son of Spiro the kafeneon owner, who goes fishing maybe three or four times a day when the weather allows. He brings in anything his nets can catch, and sells it in the village; from whitebait to swordfish, via red mullet, tuna and the yellow and brown speckled Mediterranean lobster. The lobster here is as expensive as in London.

Just once, Akis brought in a monster that made me jump out of my skin. I was surprised by its grin as I walked past one of his baskets on a kafeneon table without really noticing what was there. It had a head bigger than an adult human's, bulging glassy eyes and a huge and wide open sharp-toothed grin. It looked for all the world like one of the monsters in Hieronymus Bosch's visions of hell. It was probably extremely tasty, but I wouldn't like to have been the cook who had to handle it.

The diving school in the village brings back stunning colour photographs of some of the bizarre marine creatures its customers and staff encounter in the waters around Lakka. Like the village's tiny aquarium, the diving school is run on ecological lines: the aquarium returns its live

· 153

exhibits to the bay at the end of every summer, and the divers refuse to tell anyone where they dive to photograph these fish, fearing that fishermen will go after them. They occasionally invite people they trust to accompany them, and I was once invited along for the ride, but as a non-diver I suspected a morning bobbing alone in a motorboat on the swell off the west coast wouldn't do my breakfast much good.

Paxos mythology even holds that Lakka was once visited by a shark, and there are some circumstantial facts that suggest this might be near the truth. I was in Lakka at the time but, given my natural tendencies towards paranoia, off the beach that day. It was late in the summer of 1988, perhaps into the middle of October. Two sailing school instructors claimed they were out on the bay on windsurf boards when it swam in below them. Privately, they said it was very probably a basking shark, large, but harmless, although the average holidaymaker isn't going to know that, still less be able to differentiate this harmless shark from the breed of shark that circulated publicly in the mythology's rumour mill: the perhaps inevitable great white. I was taken aback to find that great whites do indeed breed in the Mediterranean; one study sites them in the Adriatic, above the Ionian between Italy and the former Yugoslavia and a little too close for comfort here in the northern Ionian. They also breed in the sea between Tunisia and Italy. This makes the Ionian as popular a cruising ground for great whites as it does for flotillas. Yet not one story has circulated about great white sightings, less still attacks, although the career paranoiac only has to remember what the politicians of Amity, Martha's Vineyard, did to cover up their problem with Bruce the mechanical shark to wonder what is being said and done about the great white population of this region. Marine biologists claim that the great white has been given a very bad press, and I have seen footage of people swimming with great whites, but it also seems likely that any unwary swimmer who gets in the way of one of these things is about to meet the wrath of God with fins on and teeth in. Between them, Peter Benchley and Steven Spielberg have returned many of us to the nineteenth or even eighteenth century, when the sea housed unnameable terrors.

Lakka's shark visitor probably was a basking shark, given the fact that there were enough people in or on the bay to offer a great white a tasty mid-afternoon snack. Basking sharks are terribly docile, the folk wisdom being that they will roll over and swim off if you kick them – but boy are you in trouble if you mistakenly kick some other kind of shark! At the beginning of the century, the people of some Scottish islands, who prized the basking shark for its oil, used to wrestle them aboard small rowing boats barehanded, as recorded in Robert Flaherty's classic film, *Man of Aran*, and the sharks barely complained. Try wrestling a great white aboard a small rowing boat and you've got serious attitude on your hands.

I further believe that the Lakka shark was a basker, if indeed the thing really existed at all, because the story was talked up by sailing school instructors, who are if anything worse self-mythifiers than real sailors. It is the sort of thing that sailing school workers, enthusiasts who are paid slave wages if they want to pursue their enthusiasm for a living, would make up on a hot but boring afternoon one October afternoon in Lakka bay. Suspiciously, they were all out on the bay, with a view of this submarine-sized beast as it cruised into the bay, and some claimed to be standing stock still on windsurf boards as the monster slid finnily beneath their very own boards. It took a look around, sniffed at the odd swimmer unawares, inspected the rocks for tidbits, and ten minutes into the event zoomed back out to sea, leaving the frolickers of Lakka bay unaware of how close they had come to underwater dental apocalypse.

The Paxos great white pops up in the island's mythology from time to time, a minor but inviolate legend because those who created it no longer work on or visit the island. Those of us who were around at the time are neither able, nor, really, inclined to dismiss it. The Paxos great white is part of the magic that insures Lakka against waking up one day to find that Acapulco has landed on it.

The Paxos great white legend once made me do a terrible thing in this bay. People using high-powered waterborne toys are the bane of anywhere where people go to holiday near water. Jet-skis, in particular, serve only the rider, and offer nothing but nuisance and danger to anyone else. There have been accidental killings involving jet-skis, and there is evidence that they disrupt marine life, in particular creating radar disturbance that can separate dolphins and their offspring, often with tragic consequences.

There is only one thing worse than the jet-skier, and that is the rich asshole jet-skier. Large boats that use the bay tend to consider themselves above the rules that govern most visitors. Worst offenders are the huge powercruisers with no outdoor superstructure whatsoever, James Bondian craft which you might expect to have nuclear warheads trained on northern Europe. One of these huge beasts, as sleek and black as Rupert Murdoch's heart, slid into this bay one quiet September afternoon. Once upon a time, one would be fined for disturbing the siesta in Lakka. Nowadays, the crime goes unpunished, and without comment. This late September siesta, however, thanks to cloud cover over the beach and no wind for the sailors, the bay was silent.

Until, that is, a loud whirring engine aboard the motor cruiser announced activity on the perimeter of this totally enclosed sailing environment. A door in the second of its four or so storeys slid open, a crane poked out, and lowered a jet-ski into the bay. A retractable companionway down to the water emerged to allow one of the people on board, a man in his late twenties, into the water by the jet-ski. He was tanned, lithe and handsome, and looked like raw power, money and privilege reified into bone, muscle and flesh. Mummy had perhaps let him out to play with his trike, and here he was, about to meet his nemesis.

Somnolent in the garden, I got up to watch this princely vision switch on his jet-ski ignition and start to perform perfect circles around and around and around the bay on this quiet Greek afternoon. The noise vibrated through the water, through the air, through the *maquis* and the olive trees. It resonated through the village, and in bedrooms around the bay. And then the bastard fell off, and while he waited for it to stop its automatic circling around the point where he lost control, reader, I lost control. I checked the beach to make sure that no-one else was in the water, and let rip.

'Shark!' I screamed. 'Shark! Jesus Christ! SHAARK!'

The bastard froze.

FIFTEEN

EARTHQUAKE

THIS ARCHIPELAGO follows a seismic faultline that rises near the top of the Adriatic and hugs the coastline of Albania and Western Greece all the way down to Kythera at the bottom of the Ionian, where the faultline takes a left and sidewinds across the Aegean towards Turkey and the Middle East. The faultline would explain the fairly continuous ribbon of islands that follows the mainland from the Dalmatians off what used to be Yugoslavia, and the more erratic Eptanisa, the seven islands of the Ionian chain. As recently as 20,000 years ago, the top half of the Adriatic was dry land anyway, and most of the islands off Split and Dubrovnik landlocked. The upheavals that inundated and closed off the Mediterranean basin, and which tantalisingly offer themselves as evidence to followers of the Atlantis legend, probably produced the Mediterranean which, give or take 20,000 years of upheaval and erosion, we know today. At some point in the past, these islands were probably torn from or parted company with the mainland, or were stranded by rising seas. There are even apocryphal stories which suggest that the horseshoe bay of Lakka is in fact all that remains of the cone of a volcano that blew up millions of years ago. The fantastic folds and striations in the rock around the bay, looped and curled with the ease with which a baker might fold dough, suggest tremendous movements in the distant past.

The faultline's main area of stress is in the region of Ithaca, Lefkas, Zakinthos and Kefallonia. No less than three tectonic plates meet in this region; the Eurasian Plate, which carries Italy, much of Greece, the former Yugoslavia and other countries to the north, the Turkish-Hellenic Plate, which carries Turkey, Cyprus and the majority of the Aegean Islands, including Crete and volcanic Santorini, one of the sites of the Atlantis legend, and the African Plate, which supports most of the southern Mediterranean. They butt up against each other in the sea off Preveza. Major earthquakes have been recorded in the region ever since travellers and explorers began visiting it. Historian Michael Pratt writes in his *The Ionian Islands* that the first recorded big tremor hit Zakinthos in 1514, followed by Kefallonia in 1636 and again in 1765. An earthquake accompanied by a tidal wave hit the island again in 1867. More quakes followed in 1897-8, 1903, 1910 and 1948. Not as violent as the San Andreas fault, perhaps, and situated in a farflung region of the sparsely populated Ionian, but still a very active fault.

The fault announced itself to the world on 9 August 1953, when an enormous tremor, unmeasured on the

Richter scale, hit all three islands of Zakinthos, Kefallonia and Ithaca at midday. The Venetian architecture that had won Zakinthos the nickname of the Venice of the Ionian was flattened, never to be rebuilt, and a fire later traced to a taverna demolished in the earthquake ravaged the capital. Michael Pratt reports that entire villages disappeared in some of the hill and mountain communities, and that the American, British and Israeli Navies came to the assistance with men and supplies. Over seventy per cent of the buildings on the three islands had been destroyed, and the coastline of Zakinthos was actually altered by the force of the earthquake, stranding a bridge out at sea. Contemporary photographs from the Kefallonian capital of Argostoli, of streets with great vents in them and road surfaces heaped up like waves, suggest that the force of the tremor was about that of the San Francisco earthquake of 1904. Over 600 died in the earthquake, and 2,300 were injured, 800 seriously. Fractional figures compared to the deaths in San Francisco, but on the three islands this amounted to a terribly high percentage of the population.

Paxos, like Corfu and distant Kythera, is rarely hit by major earthquakes, although it regularly experiences small ones. I reckon I have lived through two and a half earthquakes that I knew about – discounting, that is, tremors here and at home in England too tiny to discern. The half of an earthquake is, I confess, a moot point. A minor earthquake hit San Francisco while I was there in 1986, during the night but big enough to make the top of the news. Unfortunately, I was out of town the night the earthquake hit, but my luggage survived that seismic cataclysm, even though it couldn't quite be said to have lived to tell the tale.

The first earthquake that I was around for reached me in this garden on Paxos one autumn afternoon, from a region unknown but presumably somewhere south in the Ionian in the Ithaca-Zakinthos-Kefallonia hotspot. An earthquake originates at the place where tectonic plates, the skateboards on which continents and other land masses ride, bump against each other, sometimes slipping over one another or forcing the land masses above them upwards. This energy surges upwards from miles below the earth's surface, causing its thin skin of rock and soil to rip and tear. The energy radiates out in concentric circles from the point where it reaches the surface, the epicentre.

I was sitting reading in the garden, while Graham took a decidedly unearned siesta. Sometimes, our visits to the garden, admittedly after periods of often harrowing hard work, consist of little more of going to bed and getting up in time to doze in the garden and go back to bed again. These sleep patterns can even become interchangeable. Some late autumns, when the end of the siesta period really is indistinguishable from early morning, I have been known to stagger up and make a bowl of muesli while other people are thinking about their first gin and tonic of the day. (Cue laughter from my own personal Greek chorus, the wiseguys in the garden with their gin and tonics.)

At the precise moment it happened, zero seconds into the event, I was staring out at the endless movie of Lakka bay, when a distant subterranean rumbling segued into a loud explosion downstairs. Except, of course, there is no 'downstairs' under the solid rock of a volcanic caldera a few million years old. The garden seemed to stagger, and the air swayed, but before I realised what was happening it was over. I didn't quite believe it was what I would later presume it to be, but I waited for aftershocks before investigating all the other possibilities of this phenomenon. None came, at least none I felt.

The bastards who dynamite for fish couldn't have caused it, because even quite near the bay, and I have watched them working just outside it, their explosions still produce little more than a dull underwater foom and a fountain of unlucky marine lifeforms. Nor could it have been the familiar sonic effect of planes taking off into low cloud above Corfu airport, a boom that sometimes rolls down Corfu to spook the windsurfers in the bay. The noise is quite distinct, but by no means powerful enough to shake real estate seventy miles away.

The only other likely culprit would have been the Greek airforce, those heroes of the air who use Paxos as a turning point during low-level flying practice (a sentence that may well contravene Greek airforce security). Sometimes, their practice actually looks more like a supersonic game of chicken, as they come smoking out of the north, streaking ever faster ahead of the invisible line of constant explosions their flight path paints across the Ionian, flying so low over Lakka bay you can see the sun on their windscreens and lights winking in the undercarriage, daring each other to fly just high enough not to take someone's washing or chimneypot with them as they pass overhead.

An unfortunate but hilarious anecdote attaches to the Greek airforce in relation to this garden. The first time we ever encountered these Saint-Exupérys of the islands was when one suddenly appeared over the house, flying north, early one morning. There was no telltale whine out of the north, only the explosion as it passed overhead. It might, indeed, have been passing the sound barrier as it flew over. By a zillion to one chance, it passed over just at the moment when Graham was pulling the chain to flush the loo. We were standing in the garden, marvelling at this monstrous beauty screaming away to the north, when Graham appeared in the doorway, white as a sheet. As he pulled the chain, the action appeared to be bringing not only the cistern but the roof down on him as well. We all laugh about that one nowadays, although Graham didn't entirely see the funny side of it at the time.

Yet not even these hi-tech aircraft could have produced the effect I had sensed alone in the garden, unless one had crashed into the cliff below the house, and even after a boozy lunch I would probably have noticed that. It could only have been an earthquake. I made a note in my notebook of the time and date, hoping to verify the event with the British Geological Survey later, but that got filed in the unlocated black hole that spins somewhere in my study, its event horizon occasionally subsuming the contents of my desk.

The real biggie, which was really quite tiny compared to the Big Frisco Quake but was still quite large for this garden, struck early one morning towards the end of the olive season. Curiously, I had been unable to sleep for a couple of days. Normally, I would drag myself from the narcosis of sleep and siesta wondering what planet I was on. These two days I had gone to bed around midnight but woke shortly after four. This second night I lay dozing in the silence of the bay. Even the sea had stilled to the extent that it wasn't playing its snare drums among the rocks below the house.

Perhaps I had unconsciously heard the Tone, the seismological music of the spheres which is said to presage an earthquake. This subsonic tone, presumably the vibration in the rock and magma created by the increasing tension at the point where the tectonic plates are buckling against each other, is said to have been the warning that made all the animals in Atlantis creep away into the countryside knowing that the apocalypse was upon them. The animals were attuned to hear it, but alas the Atlanteans weren't.

Joan Didion uses this device, what she calls the harmonic tone, in one of her novels of dislocation and spacey neurosis in some fetid Central American republic. In her novel, the harmonic tone always sounds when impending tragedy looms. Luckily, I was too tired to remember that bit from Joan Didion.

The clock said 5.09. I had been dozing but resurfaced into waking again. I was annoyed at waking up again so early and after so little sleep. A fishing boat seemed to be leaving the bay. The fishing boat, however, was under the floor of the house. The deep distant rumbling I could hear, a noise like subterranean turbines, grew louder and louder. Gently, the house began to tremble, and then shake. I heard it first: doors, lintels, window frames, making what seemed like a rustling, or very quiet rattling noise, as the house trembled on its foundations. I lay in bed, watching as the structure seemed to shimmer minutely, and objects around the room began to move, but again making only a light rustling sound, a sound that begged to be called a tintinnabulation. I wasn't scared, but rather fascinated. Particularly by the door, unlocked and slightly ajar, which was jiggling the metal in its lock cylinders. The rumbling rose to a pitch that couldn't have been a boat, certainly no boat small enough to enter the bay, climaxing in a sharp but muffled report, and then dying away like music. All this happened in less than a minute.

I leapt out of bed and ran outside to see what could be doing this, and to see if anything was still happening outside. Lakka Bay and its environs had fallen silent again. The sea was flat but ruffled, and played its brushes on the rocks, but no boats moved in the sea around the bay. No aircraft could be seen. No telltale hum of the dynamiters' boat engine sounded below the house or outside the bay. The circumpolar stars had snuck around to their pre-dawn position, with the Great Bear upended over the bottom end of Paxos. The sky was clear. I was alone, wide awake, naked, and probably the only human at large on the island. A faint breeze, unusually warm for this time of the morning, played off the land into the bay, but the only other sound was the tiny half-noise of the dwarf yellow and white olive blossoms detaching themselves from the trees and falling around me like snow. (As I write, a day after the Big Lakka Quake of '94, the star-shaped olive flowers are still drifting down to decorate two sleeping cats, mendicants in this garden, comatose in the unseasonally fierce May heat.) I padded back to bed, bemused but fairly certain that this had been my second Paxos earthquake.

No one else had felt the Big Shaker, but then it was very unlikely that anyone would have been up to notice. Visitors awake at that time tend to be people who have yet to go to bed, and whose faculties tend to be impaired by the things they have been doing since the time they should have gone to bed. Islanders awake at that time, and they would be few indeed, would have been preparing for work. The British Geological Survey could neither confirm nor deny that a tremor had happened in the region at that time on that day, although it did confirm that there were over eight earthquakes in the region around the period, two located in the Ionian Sea, and two between Greece and Albania, all registering between 3.0 and 5.3 on the Richter scale. Ultimately, I have to say, love me, love my apocryphal earthquakes.

And I have got rather fond of them, as one might of a memory of visiting somewhere strange or doing something unusual. The Big Shakers of Paxos remind me that this garden, this island, though they might seem to be as still, sound and solid as rock, are as shaky as that metaphor, and literally. Far underground, beneath these breathtaking folds of rock, the Mediterranean, like Europe, like the continents and supercontinents, is constantly on the move, although in measurements imperceptible to man. And as we go about our daily lives, picking olives, falling asleep in this garden, imagining earthquakes, Paxos is surfing along with them.

SIXTEEN

SEA MUSIC

A S A NEIGHBOUR to this garden, Caliban, once said, the isle is full of noises. Had he existed outside Shakespeare's imagination, Caliban would certainly have known about this island, might even have visited it. The noises he was referring to were more supernatural phenomena, specifically, we are led to believe, on Corfu, but he could have been talking about anywhere on Paxos, which is alive with a vast catalogue of tiny noises, never quite falling into total silence (which, as John Cage taught us, doesn't exist anyway).

In fact, the Paxos landscape itself might be a score by Cage, given his affection for stones, rivers and constellations as markers for his strange and magical compositions. One of the most beautiful pieces I ever heard by this mischievous genius was 'Inlets', a piece for water and fire. Musicians manipulated large conch shells full of water near microphones that amplified the amniotic gurgling over taped sounds of an autumn woodland fire. The piece unwittingly approximates the sounds of a night alone on the beach on Anti-Paxos.

One can only imagine what Cage might have made of this place. The woody hills and valleys are a living compendium of noises: the papery rustle in the crowns of the trees, the creak of ancient branches, the soughing of the wind, the manic razzing of the cicadas, goat bells, the million different voices of the sea, noisy weather, the sounds houses make, animals in the grass, birds in the air, car hooters, the rattle of halyards in the harbours, motorcars, children, doors, chairs, glasses on tables, cutlery, cooking, church bells, gunfire, the eerie slow-motion patter of olives falling throughout the olive groves, our heartbeat, our breathing, our feet on the earth.

Music plays a large part in the life on this clifftop. Don danced classical ballet as a young man, and moved into Broadway musicals when a dancing injury forced him to abandon ballet. Graham is a composer and bandleader. I have spent almost all my adult working life earning a living from writing about music.

We don't always agree on music, however. Graham and I will sometimes return to the house after a walk or errand before lunch and find Don blasting Bizet or Delibes into the bay at a volume which, up here, makes it impossible to hear yourself talk or think. Given the position of the house, and its position in the trees, little if any of this noise actually leaks out to be heard by anyone in the village or bay.

Left alone, I am likely to fill the garden with anything from Philip Glass to the KLF, via Miles Davis and Satie, although at a far lower volume than Bizet or Delibes.

Graham, if he listens to music on external speakers, is more likely to opt for Duke Ellington, or Miles Davis. Quietly.

We compromise. I like the classical music Don plays, and we both like k d lang and New Order. Listening to music in the garden while reading or sunbathing, I tend to use headphones. Remembering that I once spoilt someone's Christmas by having to review an album by the controversial art-terrorist group Throbbing Gristle on their headphone-less stereo, I am acutely aware of the differences in people's tastes. I have developed a library of tapes that more or less stay in a zip-up bag for transportation to and from Paxos: Kid Creole and the Coconuts, B52s, New Order, Grace Jones, Shriekback, Orbital, U2, Miles Davis (I once saw a woman being seasick over the side of the *Kamelia* while still listening to Davis's *Decoy*), Brian Eno, Talking Heads.

There are very special Paxos records. Davis's *Kind of Blue* is one, as is Wayne Shorter's *Native Dancer*. A personal favourite is *The White Arcades*, by West Coast minimalist Harold Budd. To me, this music evokes the olive groves in the rain, although perhaps this is because that's what I was staring out of the window at when I played it over and over at the Villa Collapso that stormy October.

The greatest, for me, is a solo recording by the pianist Keith Jarrett. I haven't liked Jarrett's solo work in the past, and still consider his coffee-table masterpiece *The Köln Concert* to be shamefully self-indulgent. A few years back, however, Jarrett recorded a solo improvised concert in Vienna, and was so excited by what he heard on playback that he called a press conference to announce that his new recording had finally achieved the level of expression that he had sought throughout his career. Jarrett is a driven perfectionist, and one with a problem; he is, apparently, wracked by almost constant pain from incurable back problems. That someone with such a condition can produce work like Jarrett's at all is remarkable. But his *Vienna Concert*, recorded, perhaps tellingly, just after the pianist had recorded some Shostakovich pieces, is a work of genius. Hearing it for the first time I was so stunned I had to go and listen to *The Köln Concert* and other earlier Jarrett recordings again to see if I had missed something. There is one brief, quiet passage in *The Vienna Concert* where the positioning of just two notes is so chilling it is almost as though Jarrett has glimpsed the end of the universe.

I played this one December morning while starwatching in the garden, with the storm coat finally doing some work and a mug of Mocha coffee against a pre-dawn chill so cold it bit at the ears and nose. It was still so dark that the water in the bay was indiscernible in the darkness. Gradually, purple then red and orange and yellow light began to spill down off the Pindos Mountains in the east, and the mountain range took on a silhouette as the darkness in the bay began to drift away. As the stars winked out, Corfu appeared, and the promontory on the other side of the bay. The sea between the islands turned grey then blue and white, and as the sun rose over the mountains, too far south for me to see until late in the morning, the familiar play of light, depth and reflection began in the mouth of the bay. Standing in this cold dawn, alone on the promontory, I could have been the last person on the planet. Listening to Jarrett's stately, elegant and terrifying music in this setting was an unforgettable experience, like looking into the heart of darkness.

SEVENTEEN

LIGHT OVER WATER

THE WATER IN THIS BAY looks different every time you
glance at it. Like the view of Corfu to the north, it is
constantly changing. Some mornings, like this one, when
patches of blue sky around six o'clock promise another
sunny day in paradise, the water is so silky smooth that
when a newly-painted blue and brown caique leaves the
bay, it is accompanied by its perfect mirror opposite, sailing
along beneath it, upside down but visible through the undulating blue-tinted mirror of the water's surface. Breezes
sometimes ruffle the surface into the texture of shot silk and
ciré, and currents stain it with long looping swatches of
darker material. Sunlight bouncing off the rocks on the
outer promontory of the bay bleeds slicks of cream into the
blue jelly, and cumulus clouds piling miles above Corfu are

reflected in the Steno Paxon strait with all the clarity and light of a strong winter sunset over the sea.

Light over water. This double abstract once inspired the composer John Adams to write a symphony about the effect. There is a particular effect that light and water have here, tellingly on mornings when we are preparing to leave (perhaps because we have to get up so early), when a patch of water across the bay gleams so ridiculously still and the rocks above it begin to glare with sunlight that the sight of those inviting turquoise depths fills me with an ineffable sadness. It is in the lee of the headland, where waves and currents coming into the bay are snagged on the rocks at the tip of the promontory, leaving this small patch of water unusually placid. Then a breeze will come and ruffle its surface, sending streams of wavelets that crosshatch the sea. As the wind rises, streams of different blues and whites streak the sea between here and Corfu like an everchanging watercolour. Corfu looms and recedes in the sea mists, sometimes rearing up in stark brown clarity, on days when local legend claims that this clearness of sea vision is an omen of bad weather. At other times it disappears behind banks of sea mist altogether, or, on days when the water nearer Corfu is lighter in colour than the water near Paxos, the larger island appears to have taken to the air, floating there like a vast and improbable dirigible tethered off Epirus. Ominously, on some occasions we have sighted pollution, a faint brown skrim hung loosely on the horizon between the northern tip of Corfu and the sea horizon below the heel of Italy. The kindest interpretation one can put on what mankind is doing to this ocean is that it is afterburn from jets taking off from Corfu airport drifting trapped beneath a barometric high. A more likely interpretation would be that industrial and automobile pollution from Italy, Greece and its

Adriatic and Ionian neighbours is marching on Paxos.

Corfu also acts as our own toy weather laboratory. On some stormy summer nights, it turns the sky over the northern Ionian into one vast cloud chamber, and there are photographs of storms to the north of Lakka where the number of lightning strikes begins to resemble the famous photograph of an electrical storm above Mount Wilson observatory. Yet, as we have proven empirically, and quite literally with footwork, these storms leave us Paxophiles time to finish our dinner before beginning to worry about the weather. One late September evening in the early 1980s, we sat down to eat dinner outside a taverna with a clear view straight out to sea. We'd barely ordered when a spectacular storm began to unfold over Corfu, with multiple varicoloured lightning strikes veining the air between the clouds and the land. Newcomers to the island, we first discussed abandoning our meals and making a run for it around the village and harbour and up the hill to safety. After a minute it became apparent that no-one else was moving, and that the storm wasn't moving towards us. A lucky quirk of geology, and one that has proved itself time and time again, seems to result in the effect that most bad weather originating in the north or east tends to hug the mainland and Corfu, although larger weather systems will sweep right across the Ionian. Yet Paxos seems to get only a fraction of the storms, and the cloudy days, that Corfu sees.

Weather from other directions is an entirely different matter. The area from the north west to the south is open sea, in the south-west until as far as Africa, which sends Paxos parcels of the Sahara in sirocco winds which paint anything left outdoors a pinky orange-red colour. This occurs when highs lift tons and tons of sand from sandstorms up into the atmosphere and send it north in weather fronts. It is this sort of weather that makes the west coast of the island so dangerous, although any bad weather will make the west coast a treacherous place to be. Where the mainland usually gives a warning of what might or might not be coming your way, in the form of piling cumulonimbus, or simply in the frag, streaks of rain hanging from storm clouds, the west coast can magic up bad weather in a matter of minutes. It can be a black cloud that suddenly appears over Anti-Paxos, sprinkling rain on your projected destination, or it can take the form of a freak squall that hops over the bay and drowns your lunch. One such local disturbance surprised us on a sunny September afternoon, announcing itself with a roaring wind and low black cloud surging over the lighthouse on the other side of the bay. We were soaked before we had time to grab our plates and run indoors. Peering astonished out of the rain-lashed windows, we watched garden furniture being blown about beneath trees and vegetation bending away from the force of huge winds. Minutes later the sun was back out, drying a garden that was dripping as though it had just emerged from the sea.

The Ionian, particularly the Ionian below and beyond Vasilatika, is a place where you can watch textbook theories about the weather being acted out for real. Pockets of warm air rise over the sea, some of them carrying spinning parcels of birds, and when they meet colder air they begin to produce moisture, which in turn becomes the fluffy mist we know as cloud. As the cloud rises, it meets more cloud. Depending on certain conditions – temperature, wind speed and direction, local depressions or highs, following weather systems, the amount of water in the cloud, electromagnetic charges between the particles inside the cloud – this cloud can do any number of things. It can continue rising to be shredded into cirrus by fast winds high in the atmosphere, denoting a change in the weather in the next day or two. This weather may, however, be over a thousand miles away, and could change direction at any moment. It could get caught between two layers of air, blotching the sky with pudding-like cumulo-stratus. It could spin out in the manner of candy floss to produce larger and larger fluffy cloud, towering cumulus, which can be taller than the tallest mountain on earth, with a base just as high, and castellated cumulus can flatten out and darken at the top, in the familiar anvil head that can spell trouble for those of us below.

The types of clouds that unfurl above the sea below Vasilatika were named in the early nineteenth century by a barber, Luke Howerd, who posited three basic types of cloud: cumulus, heaped or piled cloud; stratus, layered cloud; and cirrus, a tuft or filament. Howerd added further pre- and suffixes, such as alto, for high, or nimbus, for rain-holding, even though its root is in the Latin for cloud or radiance. Permutations on these terms – alto-stratus, cumulo-nimbus – help define the gradations between Luke Howerd's three main types of cloud.

When Howerd's clouds turn mean, they dump untold thousands of tons of water, water that has been here since the earth cooled, and which has remained in the cloud-rain-evaporation-condensation cycle for millions and millions of years. Not only do fish fuck in it, as the old joke goes, mankind has probably passed much of the planet's water through its collective urinary tract in the brief period between learning to walk upright and landing on the moon. This is perhaps one of the downsides of pantheism: somewhere out there is Jesus Christ's pee, and also Adolf Hitler's.

Whoever's it is, it falls at a steady sixteen feet a second, a little slower when it is blown sideways in storms and hurricanes. As Joan Didion's *White Album*, and Roman Polanski's *Chinatown*, have pointed out, in some places water and access to water can be a matter of life and death, for the society as well as the individual. The economic survival of whole cities, regions, islands, can depend on the availability of water.

There must have been a time in Paxos's history when its few artesian wells were sufficient to supply its small population. As its histories show, the island has been nearly depopulated by vengeful attackers on more than one occasion, and it has taken the arrival of a variety of outsiders to repopulate the island. The small community of shepherds who built the church at Ozias, which is dated around the sixth century BC, would presumably have found and used these waters. As the island's population ebbed and surged, savagely reduced by incursions and famine, the water supply seems to have remained stable, with the exception of droughts; one, in the eighteenth century, was so drastic that it is recorded in the history books as killing hundreds of islanders.

There are over eighteen reservoirs in the main villages on the island, and perhaps dozens of smaller wells in the hamlets that spot the hills. The first reservoir was begun near the church of St Apostoli, high on the cliffs above Erimitis, in 1808. It comprises a sunken tank with a concave roof designed, as are the reservoirs built today, to catch the winter and spring flood rains. It took the arrival of an English administration a few years later for a vigorous programme of reservoir, drainage, road, harbour and public building construction to begin. Under this administration, the island also began to develop an education system, and also a basic judiciary.

When the winter rains arrive, they come with such force

that dry gullies across the island become raging torrents. Much of this water is wasted, but a vast new reservoir below Vasilatika, the size of a couple of football pitches and perhaps 100 feet deep, should revolutionise domestic life at this end of the island next year. At present, the only piped water on the island is *glypha*, desalinated sea water that can only really be used for washing: if accidentally used in food preparation, *glypha* can prove to be a powerful emetic.

The islanders wait for the first winter rains to wash their roofs clean of the detritus and dust of summer, and then connect their gutters to the *sternas* in their gardens. A few big storms can fill one of these room-sized tanks with enough water to last a family the summer. One winter a few years back, Don heard an ominous swooshing noise in his garden during a particularly long storm, covered himself in waterproofs and peaked outside to find a waterfall in his garden: the storm had filled his *sterna* to the extent that it was gushing out of the overflow. This is news to celebrate with a party.

Other years, the winters have been so bad, meaning, in fact, so dry, that spring visitors have been surprised to find the water tanker ship *Panormitis* moored in Lakka harbour, its gunwales barely above the water, pumping fresh water it has brought from the mainland up into the main *sterna* above Lakka.

This should all end when, winter rains willing, the new reservoir fills with sweet rainwater, and starts pumping it through the *glypha* pipes in the spring of 1995. The reservoir should, in fact, have come on-line in 1994, but the fierce early storms of November 1993 caught the builders unawares. The reservoir, only partly completed, began to collect the rainwater, until a section of wall collapsed, sending a river of mud a foot high rolling through Lakka. The tide mark is still visible in properties that didn't have the slotted protective barriers in place in their doors.

Life in Lakka will alter drastically, but discreetly, when the reservoir comes on-line, although it will take islanders some time to change their attitudes to water, having spent so much time measuring out their lives if not in coffee spoons then in cups and pots and buckets. In the meantime, before it disappears underwater for ever, this vast stone hole hidden in the forest below Vasilatika is probably the best place on Paxos to observe another form of light over water, a box of stars, a vast everchanging window the size of a few football pitches, sliding across the heavens.

EIGHTEEN

METEOR

T HEY BECOME VISIBLE AT NIGHT, beginning around eleven and going on into the small hours, although actually they are passing through the atmosphere around the clock. One or two heralds will streak across the sky from the east, faster than the Greek airforce jets that sometimes scream overhead, and seem to slow down before they burn out, fade and appear to 'fall'. As the meteor shower grows, more and more will flare out of the east, like high-speed tracer-fire being shot over the Pindos Mountains. They appear more and more quickly, sometimes appearing quite literally in showers, and race in all directions, rather like a starburst or firework display. They are the annual Perseid meteor show-ers and they visit the northern hemisphere during the second week of August each year, as they have done since the Swift-Tuttle comet was first snared by the sun's gravity field thousands of years ago. There are another twenty other major meteor showers, one or more for every month of the year barring March, each associated with a particular comet, and each appearing to radiate out of a particular constellation – the Leonids from Leo, Taurids from Taurus, Ursids from Ursa Major, and so on – as that point in the night sky is where our quadrant of the atmosphere intersects with the tail of the comet as the earth passes through its wake. Most comets circle the sun in elliptical fashion, and have a period of anything from 76 years (Halley) to 120 (Swift-Tuttle) or more between the time when they are closest to the sun and the time they are farthest away. Swift-Tuttle came nearest to the sun on this run in 1981, and is now travelling further away, although we continue to pass through its dust trail. It reaches aphelion in the 2040s and turns for another spectacular fly-by with the sun and its observers on earth around the turn of the twenty-second century.

The Perseids, so named because they appear to shoot out of the region of the constellation Perseus, are in fact tiny fragments 'falling' off the tail or coma of the Swift-Tuttle comet, no larger than a speck of dust, but specks of dust that are travelling at such high speeds – anything between 25,000 and 160,000 miles an hour – they flare more brightly than any stars when they fly through the earth's atmosphere. The hurtling object is a meteoroid, the visual event, its streak of light, barely a few metres across but 14-20 miles long, is the meteor, and if it makes it to the ground it becomes a meteorite, hence the geological suffix. They generally enter the atmosphere at about 50 miles up, and it is interesting to compare the dark speck an aeroplane will present flying at, say, 10 miles above ground and the intense point of light a particle the size of a grain of sand can produce 40 miles higher.

This year, in the lee of the olive crop, the Perseids were far more low-key than in previous years. I stayed out meteor-hunting in the garden until dawn some nights, nights when the unbelievable temperatures of the heatwave that had gripped the island since Easter sent balmy waves of heat rolling across the garden at four-thirty in the morning. It was, in fact, even possible to sleep out in the garden, stretched out on a garden lounger, in shorts and T-shirt, as it appeared that either the heatwave or the season itself had done for the mosquitoes. I survived my meteor hunts with only a few deliciously itchy bites.

The Perseid meteor season, of course, occurs at the unloveliest time on Paxos: mid-August, that mythic season of vast crowds, rude Italians (and ruder waiters), high prices, flaring tempers, and that beating, beating sun. Well, the sun certainly beat down, and the prices were high, putting the prices in some places on a par with London's West End, but there were no crowds, few rude Italians, and, consequently, fewer people for the waiters to be rude to. There were plenty of people on the island, friends told me, but they were staying in at night and fleeing to isolated corners of the island during the day. A boat trip down the east coast revealed people clinging to every available cove, rock and cleft in the rocks, a crowd strung out along the Paxos littoral like improbable refugees clad in designer leisurewear. For the ostentatious Italians to be joining the Pummaro and tagliatelli brigade, and I stood in Spiro's mini-market and watched them, seemed to be another little factor that lent itself to the theory that Paxos's tourism economy, like its climate and like its olive crop, was spiralling slowly out of control.

None of the islanders I spoke to had ever heard of or seen

the Perseids: the sky was part of the roof, something that was just there, although clearly they knew about shooting stars and even the names of constellations. One night, back in the winter, driving south with Pano, we turned a corner and were jumped by Orion, sprawled breathtakingly across the southern sky. If it had really been the hunter up there, he would have been flying east, on his side, like Superman zooming across the sky, although this Superman would be a few billion miles 'high': Betelgeuse, the flaming red giant in his shoulder, is estimated to be 250 million miles in diameter *on its own*. Startled, I exclaimed, 'Orion!' and pointed. '*Neh, neh,*' Pano nodded, glancing up and returning, disinterested, to concentrate on his driving. Clearly, these stars were part of his outdoor furniture, along with the olive trees and the sea vistas, beautiful, but unremarkable.

Pano was baffled by the notion of the Perseids, although in his travels he has seen more than his fair share of shooting stars. In fact, I was probably one of the few people on the island keeping an eye out for them. Steve, who had sailed north to an island off the top of Corfu with his partner Polly, would probably look for them on their borrowed 45-foot ketch – amusingly, a vessel obviously christened by a Star Trek fan: *The Stardate* ('Captain's Log, stardate...') – but most other sightings from Paxos would probably be accidental.

The meteor hunt yielded a poor crop this olive year; mist and partial cloud cover (which reflected the heat back to earth, making the nights so infernally warm) obscured much of the action. But most nights they came, sporadically, flaring in sublime arcs overhead. The nights began with a gaseous orange full moon hanging low in the west, giving the entire sky a weird science fiction aura, like you'd imagine sunset on Mars, and when it finally sank the sky was kept from turning inky black by the man-made aurora borealis beaming up into the night sky from the various resorts on Corfu. Most nights ended with a milky dark-blue sky burning off as the fierce heat of the sun began its eight-minute journey to the garden.

Unlike the winter nights when I could have been the last man on a cold and dark planet, I had plenty of company on these meteor hunts. Loud Italian conversations often drifted across the sultry headland until two or three in the morning, and the height of the meteor showers coincides with the Name Day for Greek men called Christos, occasioning many wild parties, one of which played ersatz 1950s rock-'n'roll loudly on the beach in the bay until the sun came up. I had no trouble staying up until dawn that night. But conditions conspired to keep me from netting the big one, a meteor I have dreamed of seeing for nearly two decades.

It is, I'll readily confess, a fictional meteor, one that was captured in a painting on a record sleeve for an album by Weather Report, *Mysterious Traveller*, of what looks like a star making a suicide plunge down a starry blue-black night sky above a jungle waterline, its trajectory reflected in inky black jungle waters. I have visited a similar jungle night scene, and watched its sunset from that dugout on the edge of a lagoon in a mangrove swamp on Mexico's southerly Pacific coast, but no dying stars fell out of its sky. Its improbably long flare is transfixing, a stellar kamikaze mission into a landscape out of Henri Rousseau. I have the landscape, and Paxos is the likeliest place for me to find that meteor. If I could catch that falling star, the image would be complete. At least, if there's one thing these stars over Paxos teach us, it's patience.

NINETEEN

GOD SLOT

A<small>S WE LOUNGE AROUND</small> under this million-year-old starlight, some of which began its journey towards this garden before things began to crawl out of the seas on earth, it is perhaps inevitable that the name of God crops up now and again. He, or she, is one of the topics that we find ourselves getting around to when we're enjoying ourselves too much talking in the garden and don't want to go to bed.

We number two atheists and one agnostic. The last is me, an illegitimate orphan placed in a Roman Catholic orphanage, happily adopted by a large, loving family but forced, by law, to be brought up in the religion of my biological parents (an irony that I have had time to savour). Like the Jesuits, the Catholics get their nails in early, and deep, and no manner of rationalisation, no witty aperçus about not being able to empirically disprove what it is empirically impossible to prove, namely the existence of this Catholic deity, can dislodge the remaining vestige of Godism stuck in some superstitious corner of my brain.

I actually left Catholicism at the age of twelve, when an RI teacher told my class that it would be easier for a camel to pass through the eye of a needle than for a bastard to enter the gates of heaven. He probably didn't realise he had at least one bastard in his class, but presented with such information I saw no point in staying in the queue to get into his heaven. I became the first Marxist in Britain whose parents still made him wear short trousers.

The problem is, Catholicism hasn't left me. An improbable dream some years ago had me involved in a shootout on an American highway. We killed a cop, dumped the body and hid out in a roadhouse. We were missing only Ida Lupino and her little doggy from the final reels of *High Sierra*. I had been shot in the chest, and was holding a handy piece of medical lint against the wound. The piece of lint, an image no doubt dredged up from the memory of a B movie on Sunday afternoon TV, was probably the strangest part of the dream: what sort of ruthless killer packs a First Aid kit? It soon became apparent from the amount of blood seeping through my lint that I was going to die. As the question, What if there really is a heaven and hell? crossed my gunman mind, I woke up swearing. This choice example of Roman Catholic mind control will be with me on my deathbed.

This isn't the only reason I despise organised religion. A few hundred miles north of this garden, in the former Yugoslavia, Christians and Muslims are ripping a country apart as I write these very words. Their religions are mowing down the people who flock to their churches and mosques, laying waste to their cities, towns and countryside, and torching what little chances they have of economic recovery. Scorched earth barely begins to describe what the victors are likely to inherit. You have to fly over, or near, this war if you go on holiday to Greece. Victims from the war, and the 'ethnic cleansing' that is now spilling over into Albania, are turning up at the general hospital in Ioannina, the capital of Epirus, an hour and a half by bus from Igoumenitsa, which is opposite this garden on the mainland. When victims of war start turning up at places where you sunbathed quite recently, the war comes a little closer than the top of the news. My motto in these circumstances is scratch a pogrom, sniff organised religion.

Stephen Hawking thinks he may have glimpsed the hand of God around 45 billion years ago, which is about as far as the most powerful radio telescopes can reach into space. (He may, however, have to revise that, if recent claims that its age is only a third of that are proved.) The hand of God theory in physics and astronomy is nothing new, although interestingly Stephen Hawking concludes, in *A Brief History of Time*, that if God did build the universe, then he, or she, hasn't had a hand in it ever since lighting the blue touch-paper and retiring. I read Hawking's famous book in this garden, as it's the only place where I could regress to the reading level of a seven-year-old, following sentences with your finger and mouthing them silently to yourself to try to absorb the boggling information they contain, that reading *A Brief History of Time* required, at least from this reader. I am, alas, neither a theoretical physicist nor a theologian, but the sort of universe that Hawking describes in his book seems vastly more complex than the mind that invented Christianity could have begun to imagine. This universe, in fact, seems fantastically more complex than the minds that invented any of this planet's religions could have dreamt of, with the possible exception of Buddhism. Organised religion has, of course, been on the run from science since language and literacy began to question its fairy tales, which is why in the past it used (and still uses) its political power to persecute scientists, from Galileo to Darwin and beyond. Even though Stephen Hawking has his own religious beliefs, in his universe religions that don't allow bastards into their heavens will find their most embarrassing opposition. A universe in which time may one day run backwards, shrinking down into the infinitesimally small, zillionth of a second singularity it exploded out of, was invented by a far smarter guy than the one who invented primitive belief systems predicated on the oppression of women. It was invented by an Einstein, whereas religions which hold that people will be dragged up to heaven by their hair were invented by cavemen.

I derive some theological comfort from these Paxos nights, a safety in numbers among the millions of stars, most of which had been burning for billions of years before the Jewish boy Jesus Christ was born. Point a telescope or binoculars at the night sky and the instrument will reveal billions more stars than can be seen by the naked eye, some visible as single points, but most visible only as a dust or smoke where they cluster in the unfathomable depths of space. This was one of the first heresies committed by Galileo, who proved that space had depth and that we weren't inside some vast uniform star-studded sphere. Organised religion sent Galileo to the Inquisition to punish this intelligence.

There are over a billion stars in our galaxy alone, and it is only one of an infinity of galaxies. Our own galaxy is so large, the writer Timothy Ferris says in *Coming of Age in the*

Milky Way, that scientists estimate the average time it would take to transmit and receive messages from a solar system similar to ours in the same galaxy would be 100,000 years. We have barely had the technology for more than 100. And one day in the distant future all these galaxies may well implode into to a size infinitesimally smaller than Swedenborg's angels dancing on their pinhead.

So as we lounge around under this million-year-old starlight, marvelling at the beauty of the night sky, it seems ridiculous to think that, if a single intelligence did create all this gas and matter and radiation, it should somehow have either the time or the inclination to dislike homosexuals, single mothers or people who eat meat on Fridays. Or that it should want to issue fatwahs against writers or mutilate women's genitals for the sake of its own glorification. But the cavemen who invented these scams were devilishly clever monsters. Their cunning has left this sceptic pinning his hopes on either sudden death or coma, another irony I have plenty of time to savour.

TWENTY

FAREWELLS

A ND THEN one glorious October morning, for Paxos can be kind with its Indian summers, it is gone. There might be patches of clement weather ahead – those weeks around Christmas and New Year, that month and a half at Easter – but the summer has gone, packed up and decamped during the hours of darkness. As well as the seasonal weather, the culture of the summer – restaurants, bars, people, fresh foods, newspapers, outdoor living – is also on the wane. Lakka has begun to close down for another winter.

It most commonly occurs at a certain point down the path to the village, where it takes an abrupt turn inland, away from the weather associated with the open sea beyond the bay, and into the weather inside the bay and the valley beyond the village. Instead of the warm, fluffy air that has embraced the island for the greater part of the summer, there's a fresh breeze blowing from the south, and a cool edge to the air in the bay. It registers on the forearms, the temples and most of all between the shoulder blades. All of a sudden, there's an autumnal smell in the air, a smell of humus, overripe fruit and wood smoke. You notice from the trails of smoke curling above the houses in the hills that people have begun to light fires in their homes. Shards of mist get caught in the crowns of the cypresses, which swing around crazily in the wind. They make you think about the mad landscapes of Van Gogh's last pictures, and you begin to appreciate what he was trying to convey.

This is an especially poignant season, not least because in the past it has meant that we too were about to decamp from the island, perhaps for as long as eight months or more. There is an air of closure, and ending, and of time running out. In the background, of course, lurks the British winter, of rain-slicked London streets, and darkness at four in the afternoon. The islanders, too, have the winter on their minds, winter chores, winter work away from the tourism racket. Some even move out of the village to winter homes, usually their family's house in the hills, after the summer business has fled. Still others, like Angelo Mastoras up at his vast Villa Blotto, will close up and leave to spend the winter in Athens. Others, like Julie and Pano, will spend the winter in England. A few, those enviable gypsies with seaworthy craft and experience, will sail off for Egypt, the Canaries, the Caribbean or even the Galapagos Islands.

Despite the underlying tinge of sadness, this season has given me some of my most exquisite moments on Paxos. One autumn, when work detained Graham in London, I and Barbara snatched two weeks here in October, and it was an Indian summer. We took a boat trip to Anti-Paxos and were the only people swimming in Voutoumi bay. We threw our swimming costumes back on to the beach and spent an afternoon skinnydipping in that impossibly turquoise, impossibly warm water. I will remember that afternoon until the day I die.

All the restaurants in the village had closed by then, with the exception of the ancient Souris family taverna. At night, we sat outside, as there were no tables inside, at a table by the window overlooking the charcoal grill, huddling against it for warmth when the cool sea breeze found its way through the alleys into the square. We were its only customers, almost the only people about in the village. As the Indian summer held, we spent lunchtimes there too. Someone had left a pile of wool in the square, waiting to be carded and spun, and someone's puppy had discovered it. The puppy would roll around in the wool while we lounged in the sun, the only people in the square apart from the two Souris brothers lurking in the gloom of their kitchen. We would take two or three hours over a lunch of *taramasalata*, *tsatziki*, salad, bread, *retsina*, and more *retsina*. While the heat had gone from the air, it was still there in the sunshine, and it was possible to get sunburnt even if the air felt fresh.

The beach was ours, entirely. We could have had a door policy, a guestlist and those ropes you see outside night-clubs, but nobody came. One day, we even skinnydipped off the main beach at Lakka. If anybody saw us, they must have had binoculars, and we were too wet and happy to care.

We even outstayed the guest workers, with the exception of two senior people from the sailing school. We were on the quay one sunny morning to bid farewell to a ferry taking them and workers from Loggos and Gaios back to Corfu for their flights home.

Departures from Lakka are almost always fraught, for one reason or another. When the *Kamelia* still left from Lakka on a Monday morning, almost as many people came out to see it off as gathered in the evening to greet its return. The arrival and departure of the *Kamelia* was one of the main events in the village week. In summer and winter, it brought visitors and supplies, parcels and papers, patients travelling to and from Corfu and the mainland, sometimes even doctors and police. Canny shoppers would keep an eye on the groceries being loaded off the boat, checking for avocados, lettuce, strawberries, or anything else that might sell out within minutes of appearing outside Steve's and the mini-market. Each Monday also brought, of course, fresh waves of tourists, and the seats outside the Harbour Lights bar were the best place to check them out, looking for people you had met here before, even looking for friends or acquaintances from home: over the years, I have bumped into at least three friends or acquaintances who were visiting Paxos without knowing that I would be here, and without my knowing they were arriving. When the *Kamelia* was retired to a day-trip run between Corfu and Albania, following the collapse of the Hoxha regime, all that village culture went with it.

I had mixed feelings about the fate of the *Kamelia*. The view of Lakka from the bows of the old ferry as she motored between the promontories and into the bay was incomparable. The sight of the village receding as she motored away from it on Monday mornings became, eventually, unbearable. Those Monday morning departures attracted a large number of villagers, seeing off family or friends, or who were just nosy about who was leaving that day. They would line up on the quay – Don, Pano, Stefano Apergis, Spiro Aronis and Spiro Petrou, Pano Aronis, the Grammatikos brothers, maybe Sula and Nancy, Julie and Pano, dozens of others –

and wave at us all crammed in the back of the *Kamelia* waving back at them. People would mime clambering off the boat or diving in to swim back to Lakka. The people on shore would laugh, and smile, and as the boat left the bay turn and walk away. After one autumn departure on the *Kamelia* too many, I began to find this ritual almost impossible. I would wave, and smile, but walk away from the stern, blinking back tears, a frog in my throat I can feel now as I describe it.

That Monday morning, as we waved goodbye to a different ferry carrying its load of guest workers, it seemed as though the *Anna Maria* could have sailed to Corfu on its own tears. The cramped stern area of the ship presented the most extraordinary sight: young men and women, hair bleached and bodies browned after a summer in the sun, in tears at their imminent departure. Such occasions are often attended by irrational emotions, but they are no less raw or painful for their irrationality. Some of these young people would return, others would never come back, but the emotions they were feeling at leaving were the sort of emotions we all feel at the end of a wonderful holiday, magnified perhaps ten- or even a hundred-fold. Dave and Joanne, two of the older guest workers, staying on for a few weeks longer and more used to these sort of scenes, found themselves the focus for this outpouring of emotion.

As this tearful cargo slowly pulled away from the dock, Dave and Joanne conferred behind their hands and then returned to waving goodbye to their friends. When the ferry was safely away from the dock, they joined hands, ran up the sloped jetty and, fully clothed, leapt hand-in-hand into the sea behind the departing ship. By the time they surfaced, the stern of the *Anna Maria* was full of people laughing and cheering at this wonderful gesture. Dave and

Joanne trod water and waved for a minute or two, and then swam back to the quay. Those of us left by the jetty applauded and helped them out of the water. As the *Anna Maria* disappeared out of the bay, Dave and Joanne padded off, dripping, to dry themselves and change their clothes. With both ferry and jumpers departed, the quay seemed emptier than it had ever been before. Another lightbulb had gone off in the Paxos summer, and the island seemed to grow smaller, the light dimmer. Lakka was shrinking, the trees seemed to be pressing in on the village. Night was falling earlier and earlier, and it took longer for the sun to reach the garden. Soon, the storms would be on their way.

A few days later, when no one was looking, hoping to appease certain marine deities – Poseidon among them, I suppose – and secure a safe journey home, I performed this ritual myself, clothed in shorts, T-shirt, plimsolls, underwear, taking a long hard run at the fresh air out there a few feet beyond the jetty and landing in perhaps 20 feet of water. In fact, I cajoled Barbara into daring me to do it, as if I needed an excuse. Poseidon can't have been very impressed with this offering, for we barely got off the island. Rough seas that had inundated Gaios harbour kept the *Pegasus* in port for an hour or two after she was meant to leave. Eventually, the captain decided that the seas were relenting to the extent that the *Pegasus* could sail. After an hour and a half of rock'n'rolling through waves that made the speedboat yaw through a good 90 degrees, we made it to Corfu, just, but Poseidon had some other tricks up his sleeve. Returning to London, I found I'd lost my job.

TWENTY ONE

CHRISTOS ANESTI

T HESE ARE THE TWO MOST IMPORTANT WORDS in the Greek
religious and social calendar: literally, Christ is risen.
They are uttered by priests on the stroke of midnight on
Easter Saturday, ushering in a new year, a day of feasting,
and a week of celebrations marking the end of the winter
that begins, like that day on the jetty, on the last day of
every summer season.

The Greek Easter rituals also have a hint of the primitive
festival of new fire, and on Corfu Easter Saturday is marked
by a bizarre ritual where households in the centre of the
town dump their old pots out of the window at eleven in the
morning, filling the street with exploding urns, jars and
other earthen kitchenware. This has been interpreted variously as representing the stoning of Judas Iscariot, the

breaking open of Christ's tomb, and a medieval, and anti-Semitic, tradition of clearing Corfu's Jewish population from the streets on this Christian holy day. It also has more than an echo, like the new fire, of the ancient practice of destroying symbolic items of property around the new year.

The Greek Easter differs from the Church of England one in that each year its date is designated by the rules of the Orthodox Church. In 1994, the Greek Easter fell quite late, with Easter Sunday on 30 April, two weeks later than the Church of England Easter, and only a day before the tourist season officially began.

The Paxos Easter begins on Friday evening, as elsewhere, with the parading of the local icons. These are portraits of local patron saints, single and in groups, covered in silver or gold, leaving only the saints' heads and hands visible. They are potent objects in the Orthodox Church, and carry the same power to heal and bestow good luck as, say, statues of the Trinity and Virgin Mary do in Roman Catholic churches. At certain festivals, they are put on display and people are allowed to kiss them for luck. On Friday evening, the icon of Lakka's main church is taken for a spin around the village by a small procession of priests, attendants and villagers. The procession is led by a young boy carrying a wooden cross taller than himself, two boys holding lighted candles, another two carrying sceptres topped with golden sunbursts, the village priest in vivid red and white robes, and a group of four village men carrying a beautiful flower-covered palanquin with the icon inside it. They in turn are followed by a group of cantors, who are still singing parts of the two-hour Orthodox mass that precedes the procession, and which will continue when the icon returns to the church. Villagers and members of the Lakka diaspora, dressed to the nines, walk along behind this startling vision.

It is a far from solemn affair; many wait outside the church for the procession to begin, chatting, smoking, calling to friends, popping in and out of the service, and even during the procession people drop out for a fag or to talk to a friend. The church itself is one of the largest on the island, with interior balconies and tiny side chapels, huge floor-standing candles, censers hanging from the ceiling, and a wealth of vulgar ornamentation. There are, however, no seats, as appears to be the case in most Greek churches.

The weather in the run-up to this Easter had been changeable, but dry. On Easter Friday, however, dark clouds brought an early twilight and threatened to turn to rain. Before the icon left the church, a few drops slapped down on Lakka, but the night remained dry. The procession marched to the quay, and the priest barked something at the waves slapping up against the stones in the thickening darkness. The procession continued on to the other end of the quay, where the priest barked some more imprecations at the sea, and then turned inland, through the farthest, and tiniest, alleyway in the village, leading through Edward Kennedy Plaza and back towards Spiro Petrou's kafeneon and the church beyond. In the village backstreets, beneath balconies, arches and stone stairways copied from the Venetian style, the flickering candlelight gave the procession a distinct air of the Middle Ages. When the icon was returned to the church, some stayed for an extension of the mass, but most drifted away to meet family and friends.

The village seemed to be full of strangers who all knew each other. You soon realize that these people, dressed in elegant and expensive clothes, are islanders who have chosen to make their lives elsewhere: on Corfu, in Athens, or abroad. Their evident wealth does not seem to present a social barrier for either them or the villagers. Some of the scruffiest men in Lakka, mutton dressed as lamb in their finest suits, were hugged by women dripping jewels and fur, and in a way I would think unlikely if the ritual were transposed to a British village of a similar size. They were, of course, conversing in a language largely alien to me, but I did not sense a class structure at work in these displays of fondness and affection. Their presence, and the evident welcome with which they were greeted, also underlined how contingent my presence is here as an interloper. Despite having fled to Athens, Amsterdam or America, this was still their home.

They were also the reason for all the fevered activity in the village in the past week or so. The tourist season wouldn't really get into gear until about two weeks after Easter, when the charter flights would begin landing at Corfu, but all the tourist accommodation in the village had been aired and cleaned in preparation for this brief invasion. One night a few days before Easter, toiling back up the hill in the blue-black evening, now no longer fearing that Jason or Leatherface would be lurking in the shadows, I turned to look back on the village, and it seemed that every room and window in the apartments and villas around the village was blazing with light. The effect was heightened by the fact that all this spring cleaning was going on with the curtains open in each room, hence the eerie light in a village that only days ago had been virtually deserted. These preparations would shift seamlessly into the village's preparations for the new season, but for the time being, with the spring airing done, Lakka, like the rest of Paxos, and the rest of Greece, took the weekend off.

On Saturday evening, everyone converged on the village again for another marathon Greek Orthodox Church service, although this one is traditionally timed to end at midnight, when the fun begins. Again, the service, while highly traditional, was also fairly informal; people popped out for cigarettes, or to have a natter with a friend, or just lounged around in the door to the church. Those who didn't feel the religious fervour necessary to actually get them as far as the church lounged in Spiro's kafeneon, dressed in Sunday best, holding the candles that would be lit from the new flame from the church, gossiping. Some seemed a little bemused at the sight of a lone Englishman, in distinctly untouristy clothes, sitting on his own drinking coffee and with the votive candle clearly sticking out of his knapsack. The metrio coffees were a precaution against falling asleep, either in Spiro's kafeneon waiting for midnight to roll round, or at Pano's, where I had been invited for the traditional Easter soup, *magaritsa*, after the mass, a meal that might well last into the small hours, as it did.

Easter signalled the start of the miniature heatwave that would last into June and beyond a brief storm into the autumn. The weather, which had rumbled a little the night before, turned cloudy again this evening. Having abandoned leather sandals, shorts and T-shirt for proper shoes, trousers and freshly pressed white shirt, I had also worn a jacket against the evening weather. There was the odd rumble as a straggle of guest workers, employees of a new sailing club preparing for the coming season, began to congregate for the midnight ritual, but as a crowd gathered on the hard dry earth outside the church, spilling on to the road out of the village, the weather seemed to be holding.

Until, with devilish timing, about five to twelve. The tell-tale patter of rain on hard ground announced a drilling downpour that sent us fleeing under trees or into the church. It seemed to be a cloudburst right over the village, and the rain fell straight down like stair rods. As midnight

struck, however, the rain halted long enough for the ritual
to take place. The village priest emerged from the church,
along with some of the congregation, while others remained
inside. The doors were duly locked against him, as the ritual
demands, and he had to knock on the doors and demand to
be let back in. Laughter erupted from the crowd around the
door, however, when his first knock made the doors fly
open, and he had to grab them and shut them again himself.
A few hard raps later, the guardians of the door let him
back in properly, and he duly emerged with a lighted candle and began to share out the new flame, although in the
rain and confusion some had lit theirs already with lighters
and matches. Some of the candles were decorated with rib-
bons and flowers, and a lot of the children's candles had
small toys tied to them. There were the inevitable mishaps,
and a faint whiff of singed material hung in the air, but there
were no accidents. As the flame, official and otherwise,
spread around the churchyard and the road, light seemed to
dance around the crowd, and this was accompanied by fire-
works, the ferocious firecrackers beloved of village children,
and gunfire. Akis Petrou and some friends lit the whole
scene with what looked like hand-held red emergency
flares. Everyone shook hands, or kissed, and wished each
other *kronia polla*, even we tourists and guest workers. This
was Lakka's small but lovely equivalent of Trafalgar Square
on New Year's Eve, when everybody set aside their differences, or at least politely overlooked them, to wish each
other Happy Easter and a long life. As people began to drift
away, the rains returned. Marianthi and Lavinina jumped
into the taxi with a neighbour, and rumbled off home, their
candles still alight in the back of the cab: if you get the candle home still alight, this is meant to bring good luck to your
home and family for the next year. Pano and I walked to his

house in the rain, along the road that winds around the village and on towards Vasilatika. It was interesting just to
watch Pano walking in the rain: where I bent against it and
hopped from beneath one tree to another, he just walked
through it as he would walk through a breeze or blistering
sunshine.

There was a blazing fire in the brick fireplace in the corner of Marianthi's kitchen with its big picture window
overlooking the beach. A large stew pot bubbled and
steamed on a gas cooker next to it. This contained the notorious *magaritsa*, the lamb's gut stew so reviled among British
visitors. The stew, or soup, is made of the offal from the
lamb, or in this case kid, that will be roasted for the big family meal the following day. While the spit-roast lamb is the
big feast, the *magaritsa* is the symbolically important meal,
breaking the Lenten fast. Villagers prepare for it days and
even weeks ahead, and on a number of occasions during the
run up to Easter an unfamiliar engine sound had drawn me
to the cliff edge only to see an islander and his wife bringing a sheep to Lakka to be killed and prepared for Easter.

I had heard enough about it to fear the *magaritsa* myself:
some descriptions suggested that it contained unmention-
able parts of the lamb's offal, including, in one apocryphal
instance, the penis. I would draw the line at sheep dick, but
after weeks of vegetarian cooking and a day of near fasting
in preparation for the *magaritsa*, I was determined to con-
quer this culinary commando course if it killed me.

Pano and Marianthi must have sensed my apprehension
as a large plate of the stew appeared in front of me: Pano
insisted two or three times that something else could be
cooked if I didn't like the *magaritsa*. Vasili and Lavinina
grinned, all too aware of the legend attending the meal.
They, of course, were highly amused at the horrified British

response to this Greek delicacy.

Here in Marianthi Vassilas's kitchen, another chapter of the Paxos mythology was turned on its head. Others may have found sheep dick and unspeakable tracts of the lamb's digestive system surfing around their plate, but I was staring down at a serving of delicately-cooked kid's liver and chopped intestines that tasted a little like the finest tripe served at Bofinger, Roland Barthes' favourite restaurant in Paris, just around the corner from l'Opéra. Marianthi's *magaritsa* consisted of pieces of liver and intestine that were too small to look like the organs that gave a name to the horror that myth associated with the meal. With bread, a horiati salad and a rosé wine made locally from Corfu grapes, it was one of the two finest meals I've eaten on Paxos. (Perhaps unsurprisingly, the other finest meal was also cooked and served in this kitchen, a lunchtime late one October, when I broke my no-moussaka rule to eat Lavinina's delicious homemade version.)

Patrick Leigh Fermor may have travelled at a time when dancing and music might have accompanied such celebrations, but we ate to the accompaniment of one of Greece's main television channels, which was broadcasting a bizarre Miss World pageant, sort of Andrew Logan via John Waters, hosted by two famous Greek comedy actors parading, rather homophobically, as preening queens. The contestants were all outsized middle-aged women in grotesque costumes and make-up. This was intercut with light entertainment slots apparently styled, like the Greek TV at Christmas, on British light entertainment from some decades ago, the 'Billy Cotton Band Show', perhaps. Famous Greek pop stars, including a young woman from Gaios, sang their latest hits, all of them in Greek. This is at least an improvement on northern Europe, where most pop hits have to be sung in mid-Atlantic English.

At around three a.m., the ugliest woman won the beauty pageant, and Lavinina announced she was going to bed. Vasili had already fled, after the meal, to a party with some friends. Thanking Pano and Marianthi, I wished them goodnight and set off for home.

The village was unusually silent. Normally, there would be somebody still carousing outside a restaurant, or forcing a bar to stay open. Yet even the hardened party animals had slunk home, and everything was shut and locked up for the night. The village was quiet, but all the business lights were on, perhaps in celebration of the holiday, giving Lakka a spookily abandoned look. The stars winked behind patchy cumulus as I climbed the hill, still feeling weirdly sober and wide awake even though it was nearly four in the morning.

The waves on the rocks below the house were making a seductive white noise that washed up the cliff face rhythmically, a noise that might sound something like the sound of a baby's blood and nervous system pulsing in the amplifying medium of amniotic fluid. Exhausted but a little spacey at the end of a day that had started twenty-two hours earlier, I curled up in bed, suddenly aware of being the only person sleeping on this hillside, this promontory, at this time of year, and let the noise wash over me.

Easter Sunday is traditionally a family day, when relatives get together to roast a whole lamb on a spit, recovering from the previous night's partying and, for some, tying on another hangover. Others, however, and Pano is among them, take to the hills with their shotguns, intent, once more, on turning the skies above Paxos into one vast shooting gallery. Gunfire is a common sound on Paxos – it is not uncommon to be showered with lead shot, walking in the countryside, or even, once, lying in a hammock in this garden – but at Easter, perhaps because the visitors have little opportunity to shoot in their city environments, the gunfire takes on an unusual ferocity. At times, with round after round blamming around the hills, echoing across the bay and up into the centre of the island, the fun begins to sound more like bush warfare.

On Easter Monday, the island's most beautiful procession takes place, walking the icon from the church at Ipapanti – said to be the most beautiful on the island – to Vasilatika and down to Lakka. The procession leaves Ipapanti, just below Circe's Grove up in the hills, at around ten in the morning, and reaches Lakka around noon.

Someone appeared to have moved Ipapanti when I tried to locate the start of the procession. I had only visited the church once before, four or five years earlier, but felt sure I knew the route up to the dusty pink and red campanile marooned up in its own secret glade in the hills. You just took a right off the main road just past the abandoned car, and hooked another right shortly after that. I hadn't reckoned on the excavations for the reservoir having shunted the car down the main road to the side of a different turning. After climbing to three dead ends, I abandoned the search for Ipapanti. At one point I thought the hunt was getting warm, and pursued a trail of trampled flowers through the olive groves, but this trail died at a fork in the path. I strained to hear the cantors singing their way through the olive groves, as I'd imagined they would – the idea of a Felliniesque religious parade through the trees was what drew me to Ipapanti in the first place, although the adjective is inaccurate, as Fellini probably stole his ideas from Roman Catholic versions of this same ritual – but all I heard was the occasional foom! of people dynamiting fish off the west coast. That, and a woman calling her husband a wanker in an argument in their garden. As I stepped back on to the main road down to the village, having abandoned the quest for Ipapanti, the bells in Ipapanti's campanile started ringing like mad somewhere up in the hills, in brute mockery of my misadventure.

Gingerly creeping past Pano's house – the embarrassment of this failure would have been too much to bear had Pano or Marianthi appeared and asked me wasn't I meant to be following the procession from Ipapanti? – I set off for Vasilatika, hoping to encounter the procession on its way down. The path and roadway were strewn with flowers from people's gardens; rosemary, myrtle, wild garlic, the fleshy cream-coloured bell-like flowers of the poisonous datura, pink, white and red carnations, velvety purple freesias, blood-red roses, the overexposed scarlets and crimsons of geraniums, the yellow-flecked pink of valerian, and the heavily scented white flowers of bush angelica. This really did look like something out of a movie: the petal-strewn sets of Paul Schrader's *Mishima*, or a dream sequence from Bertolucci or Tarkovsky. At certain turns in the road to Vasilatika, where it affords a view of the way ahead, a river of multicoloured flowers seemed to be flowing through the olive groves. It was like stepping into a Seurat painting. I don't think I have ever seen anything so beautiful in my life.

The people who had dressed this magic landscape sat outside their homes, waiting for the icon to pass. Or maybe they were making smalltalk after having watched it go past. It was approaching eleven-thirty, and I felt certain I should have encountered the procession by now. I saw Sharon and Tuli pottering about at their villa, and contemplated wise-cracking, 'Did you see an icon go by here recently?' but decided that this too bore its own admission of failure. Even a simple 'poo eenay to ikon?' would bring gales of laughter from the choirs of little old ladies gathered along the road for this very purpose. Cursing myself and by now certain that the Ipapanti icon had passed by hours ago, I abandoned the road to Vasilatika and turned back towards Lakka.

I could have bumped into anyone, but the baby Jesus decided I was going to bump into Panayiotis Vassilas, who might justifiably have begun wondering if we were sharing the same scriptwriter. Certainly, he could have believed quite reasonably that some Greek Orthodox saint had decided to supply him with his very own personal clown, namely me. He started grinning as soon as he spotted me trudging down the road. Pano was off to his secret set up in the hills for another gay afternoon of World War Two sound effects in the trees; I had at least that much over him, which made my confession of failure slightly less pathetic. He explained that the icon was fifteen minutes behind me on the road from Vasilatika, and even offered me a lift to meet it with Vasili, who happened to arrive with the taxi at that moment with a cargo of more little old ladies bound for the flower-strewn path of the Ipapanti icon. By this time I had been sweating so much my white shirt – worn, along with long trousers, because of a lapsed Catholic's warped sense of decorum – had turned see-through, at least revealing the chewing gum and Greek telephone card in the breast-pocket, and I was in dire need of a shower, a swim or a beer.

The last was the nearest to hand, and I greeted the loveliest icon on Paxos – a gathering of medieval saints, all features obscured by silver and gold bar their faces, its frame wreathed with fresh flowers and carried by a team of four men taking turns at the honour with their friends from the growing crowd that had followed it through the woods and down into the village – from the edge of Lakka harbour, where the icon, its bearers and followers paused while the priest blessed us for the umpteenth time that Easter. Small boys scattered deafening firecrackers around us, and gunfire stuttered above us in the hills. Pano must have been in heaven. The procession, with a large crowd in tow, Marianthi included, stopped again at the jetty, where the priest gave another blessing, and then the icon was carried to the church, where it would be displayed until the following Friday, when it would be carried to Loggos. The powerful smells of myrtle and angelica, released from the leaves by the feet of the devout marching behind the icon, hung around the village all day, leaking from the crushed greenery scattered through the alleyways and squares.

The following day, the visitors seemed to have vanished overnight. The village was as empty, if not as quiet, as it had been in the weeks prior to Easter. The village and environs echoed with the sound of carpentry and repair work, the banging of doors and windows as last-minute preparations were made before the summer invasion began. The few restaurants that had opened for the visitors closed again and began to prepare themselves for another season. Thick cotton awnings began to appear outside restaurants in the village square, and the familiar little flatbed truck trundled along the quayside with its yearly delivery of cut ferns for the awning over Basta's seafront bar. There were a total of six new restaurants opening this year. Akis from the pizza joint had opened his own swanky Akis bar and restaurant on the seafront at Christmas, loud with the noise of video games and snooker but with the most stylish bar on the island, all chrome and high chairs, the sort of thing Humphrey Bogart and Lisabeth Scott might have sat at in *Dead Reckoning*. The sign outside, with its gold lettering and pink neon backlight, might reasonably be said to put the LA into Lakka.

Two more restaurants were about to open within spitting distance of Akis, one mirthsomely misnamed The Albatross. A snack bar in Edward Kennedy Plaza, The Pergola, was about to reopen as a proper restaurant, offering real sirloin steaks and starters like deep-fried Brie with redcurrant sauce, things unheard of since the mid-1980s, when the Ubu Bar was probably the best restaurant on the island, and boasted the most stylish help on the island as well; Guya, a statuesque Italian beauty who cooked heavenly desserts and greeted the world with an air of elegant disdain, and Emmanuelle, a no less beautiful young French woman, who went barefoot everywhere and was last heard of working with horses in the Camargue. For a few years, the Ubu even had a real pizza oven, and a real pizza chef, until he ran amok with a chopper and had to be straitjacketed off the island. Its owner, Luciano, an enigmatic figure who works hard at this image, used to paint occult symbols on his tabletops, and everything else black and red. Named after his Pyrenean mountain dog Ubu, and presumably alluding to Alfred Jarry's *Ubu Roi*, the restaurant was also identified by an image of an Egyptian canine deity. After some Greek workmen destroyed the interior of his bar last year by accident, he left it as a bar, but decided to refurbish entirely and reopen as a restaurant. Ubu the dog died this spring. Local mythology claims that Ubu knew he was dying, and so came down from his home in the hills for a last *volta* around the village, saying goodbye to all the people he knew and all the places where he would lie down for a rest and block the alleys and the open spaces in between the tables in the restaurants.

Last but by no means least, the village's one stationer's

and newspaper shop, an Aladdin's cave of school supplies, pens, paints and paper, toys, bags, and the international newspapers and magazines, whose display could start arguments over the sole copy of the *European Guardian* delivered each day, disappeared this winter. In its place is a gleaming new restaurant. It's right next door to an existing restaurant, Horiatis, which had its services cut off last year for failure to pay taxes and bills. There are already, however, plans afoot to relaunch the restaurant by gaslight, cooking on electricity with a borrowed generator, and squatting space in a friendly rival's refrigerator to keep supplies of food and drink cool.

These six will have to compete with the existing restaurants, which had already complained at the end of the previous season that tourists, especially the British tourists, just weren't eating out like they used to. This was due in part to increased prices: the deregulation of the restaurant pricing system, which had previously been strictly enforced by the Tourist Police, who estimated just how much each restaurant could charge, has led to a hike in prices. Paxos is no longer a cheap place to eat out. The British recession, while not keeping that many tourists away from the island, had made them more cautious, and many were now eating in. There were dark mutterings about how much Spiro Aronis was making in the spaghetti and Pummaro market, and indeed one could see the tourists grazing among his shelves for the means to improvise a pasta dinner. In a moment of sheer, reckless folly, I actually mentioned this to Spiro, in a light, friendly manner, and was treated to a fifteen-minute harangue, liberally peppered with profanities, about the quality of the food in Lakka restaurants, the unimaginative menus, the fact that the owners couldn't cook, the poor quality of their ingredients, their overweening greed, and worse. Spiro's drift, essentially, was that those restaurateurs who had not been born out of wedlock were, unquestionably, compulsive onanists. We kept agreeing with him, but he wouldn't let us go until he had impressed this information on us quite forcibly.

After Easter, Lakka fell eerily quiet again. With the gloomy olive crop and a gloomy start to the season, a season that has been starting later and later in recent years, this year not until the middle of May, Lakka might have had reason to feel sorry for itself, but the village, like the island, takes these things in its stride. I'm not sure, however, how many seasons like this, how many more winters like this, that Lakka, or Paxos, can survive without some sort of radical change.

TWENTY TWO

RECKONING

W ITH EASTER GONE and the olive oil press due to close on 1 June, it comes time for a reckoning of the Paxos olive crop. This is the third year that the olive crop will produce a tale of woe, although this is at least what the islanders have been prepared through the winter to accept.

Last autumn, some casual research I did into the Greek economy and the olive oil industry produced some fantastical figures. A report on the economy of the Mediterranean reckoned that one olive tree can produce 300 kilos of olives a year. This is roughly equal to 60 litres of oil. The going rate for olive oil in Lakka this spring was around 2,000 drachmas, a little under £6, a litre. A quarter of a million trees producing 60 litres of oil each at a retail price of £6 a litre is a lot of money. If there truly are a quarter of a million olive trees on Paxos, that means that a potential £90 million falls off the trees into the nets each olive season. Where, I wondered, were they hiding all this loot?

These figures, of course, were based on the improbable supposition that there might be 15 million visitors eager to pay £6 to take home a litre of this fine olive oil. The entire Ionian, all seven of the *eptanisa* and the mainland resorts as well, receives around two million visitors each summer. Sheer geographical size and position puts Paxos at or near the bottom for the number of visitors it receives each year. In fact, the number of people present at any one time during the tourist season rarely rises above 40,000, some way short of the crowds required to generate the magical sum of £90 million income. Nor, of course, does the oil produced realise its maximum retail price. The commercial rate of selling the oil to families who produce it can be as low as 30 drachmas. A certain, not inconsiderable, percentage of the oil is returned to the olive-growers themselves without generating any cash profit whatsoever.

If they fall some way of the fabulous £90 million mark, the figures are still impressive. Andoni Argyros, Pano's nephew, runs the oil press and factory in Lakka, and is the island's agent for selling the olive oil on to Corfu, the mainland and elsewhere. A genial, bespectacled man in his forties, he speaks no English whatsoever and is a difficult man to pin down. It took weeks to arrange an interview with him with Pano acting as interpreter.

The average Paxos olive crop, in the years when it could be relied on, is around five million litres, some way short of the fantasy crop but still worth around £30 million on paper. Lakka produces around a fifth of that – six million quid garlanding the hills and valleys around this tiny village. In truth, however, the commercial rate per litre can be as little as 560 drachmas a kilo, which places the profit else-where than in the hands of the olive growers. This year, the third olive crop in succession, the total crop for Paxos will barely exceed half its normal output. Pano estimates that in some olive groves, including his own, the crop may be down to a third or a quarter of the average in recent years.

Andoni says that the yield has been roughly half the nor-mal crop for the past few years. He is at a loss to explain the recent, sudden change in fruiting patterns. Many things can affect the olive tree. Its worst enemy is the olive fruit fly, *dacus oleae*, which eats the fruit on the branch, beginning a process of decomposition that will ruin the fruit. The appetite of the Mediterranean fruit fly, *Ceratitis capitata*, will also ruin a crop. Sprays, and dry chemicals, have been employed to fight off these pests.

The olive tree can withstand a wide range of tempera-tures, from 40 degrees Celsius to -7, but that does not mean it is immune to temperature changes. A chill or winter period is necessary to aid the development of the crop, in a sense giving the tree a message to start fruiting, and while the olive tree is among the most resilient on the planet, it still needs a certain amount of rainfall to begin fruiting. Yet while recent winters have been mild in comparison with past years, none of these conditions has altered so radically as to explain the sudden change in fruiting patterns. After insects and climate, the main threat to the olive trees, says Andoni, is damage by humans. But this could hardly explain the drastic change in the harvest.

Olea Europaea is not, as it turns out, a truly biennial fruit-ing drupe. Like most drupes – any fruit, that is, with an outer skin, fleshy body and a single pit or stone at its centre – it is actually a perennial, but it's sometimes known to fall into a biennial rhythm, producing a fruit crop one year, and conserving its energies the next.

Andoni dismisses some of the wilder claims of the olive growers, that radiation from Chernobyl and other, undisclosed, nuclear accidents might be affecting the agriculture of Greece. Radiation from Chernobyl did indeed reach Greece: if television maps of the radioactive cloud were at all accurate, I probably flew through it en route to Corfu and Paxos. He will concede, however, that atmospheric pollution, and perhaps global warming, might be affecting the crop. Yet these too, are only meant to be occurring slowly, not at a speed that can transform an agricultural crop from one year to the next. At such close proximity to the freak olive crops, it is just too soon to tell what is causing the annual fruitings, and why.

So far, the disruption of the olive crop has just begun to dent the oil economy of Paxos, if only because the islanders have been alert to the freak crops and have harvested them carefully. It is difficult to estimate what long-term effect it will have, although the prognosis is bad. People like Pano, who have a variety of incomes, will survive, but others who rely on the the oil income could find themselves in dire straits. It is at times like these that single-product economies can become fatally exposed.

And in the short-term, the olive crop shows no sign of returning to its old patterns. Throughout the island, the olive trees flowered again this spring. We had to wait for the blossom to fall to see what would happen next. Up in Vasilatika, below the dry stone wall, in the sacred glades of the Vassilas olive groves, below the secret view of that ancient Greek morning, Pano's olive trees are fruiting again for the fourth year running.

TWENTY THREE

COMING HOME
(RUNNING AWAY)

T HAT WINTER'S NIGHT in Spiro Petrou's kafeneon when
Pano welcomed me 'home' was neither the first nor
the last time that I or we have been greeted in this fashion.
Once, when he had departed for England the day we arrived
on the island, Don left us a note saying the same thing, a
token, probably, of how much he knew we loved his tiny
house up in the hills. Others have also greeted us in this
fashion, part in jest, wondering how we can get any work
done between our visits to the island, part in acknowledg-
ment of our affection for the island and the islanders, or
knowing that we dream of living on Paxos. Paradoxically,
however, it seems that the more times we visit Paxos, and
the number of times must be heading for thirty now, the less
it seems likely that we will ever live here, at least full-time.

This paradox in fact masks a more profound irony, something I have also savoured at length, at moments of what I can only describe as acute alienation. Sometimes, an incident, comment or epiphany will disrupt so violently the Paxos I have constructed for myself that I begin to wonder if I even really know the place at all. I have become accustomed to the fact that the more I grow to know Paxos, the less I will ever really belong here. Islanders are privileged to do as they please on their island. We have only temporary passes. We may become liked interlopers – Don, for example, is treated as family by villagers – but we are still interlopers nevertheless. It is possible to become a part of the furniture on the island, but at moments of crisis the furniture gets moved and lines are sharply drawn. On occasion, I have even begun to have doubts about whether I should really be here in the first place.

An example of this dislocation occurred this olive winter. I was taking care of a friend's remote house, visiting to check it was okay, doing a little cleaning and tidying up. The friend's house was on the periphery of some land that was the subject of a land-grab attempt by one of the most unscrupulous businessmen on the island. I have known this islander for over a decade, a smiling, gnomish little man, whose sparkling eyes and constant chuckle seemed to convey a kindly and avuncular manner. Little did I know, as villagers later told me, that he was one of the biggest assholes in the Ionian, someone who broke civil laws with a shrug, paid his fines, and went and broke them again the same day, knowing that the law had little recourse against him, particularly in the field he found so lucrative, land sales and building.

The friend's house wasn't under threat in this man's land-grab attempt, but the path to it was. The businessman's son had been surreptitiously widening the path during the summer, 'so more tourists can come up here,' he told us, expecting to be believed. Then, one day in the late autumn, a large tree that stood on the path to the house disappeared overnight, felled and transported to make way for trucks to use the new path. At the same time, a No Entry roadsign appeared at the start of the path, intended, we were assured, to 'stop' cars trying to use the path – cars or any motorised vehicles are as likely to attempt this path as they would be to attempt the cliffs of the west coast, and in fact the sign, a red circle with a white bar across it, was intended solely to deter walkers. If the path falls into disuse, the land-grabber has greater claim to it being common land, and his opponents have less argument for making him leave the path alone or build a new one around the property he has grabbed. I have committed countless acts of vandalism against this sign, but a massive concrete base, poured to protect it against just these sorts of objections, has kept it in place.

One day in December, a pile of rocks and dead brush appeared on the path just outside the gate to the friend's house, along with a roughly-cut new 'path' through the *maquis* leading around the land the grabber had staked out. Arriving, I cleared the stones and brush and used the old path, angry but also worried that the new 'path' looked quite dangerous in places.

This game of cat and mouse went on for a few weeks, with the stones and brush returning each time I departed. Once, I had spent only a few hours at the house and left to find that someone had replaced the barrier, almost blocking my exit from the property – coincidence, perhaps, or a message. I removed it, and went into Lakka to see if anything could be done.

At this time of year, of course, the village was nearly deserted. Spiro Aronis was in his minimarket, calculator at the ready, but shrugged his shoulders apologetically. Yiorgos Grammatikos was also pottering around on the quayside, but was unable to help. It was at this point that I realised that, in certain circumstances, Paxos might appear to have been twinned with the Wild West. There is no law to protect you: no cavalry, no legislation. Even Pano threw up his hands at the situation. Not that he, Yiorgos or Spiro didn't care about what was happening, simply that there was no way of stopping it. There was, however, an unspoken subtext here. The house was in a remote part of the island where the only other properties that used the path were also owned by foreigners. It wasn't so much that islanders wouldn't do this sort of thing to each other – they would, and do, and even Pano has taken action against an aggressive neighbour's fencing off of public land – but that they could safely counter-attack in these situations, where non-islanders could not, if only because such action might make their property vulnerable, especially when they were unattended for such long periods.

Pano even took me to see the mayor about it, an example of democracy in action that I would love to see implemented in Britain. We just drove out to his house in the middle of the island, a large villa with huge picture windows overlooking the west coast, olive fire roaring in a huge stone fireplace with a set of blunderbuss-sized rifles on the chimneybreast and an open-plan kitchen off the main room, a style reminiscent of 1950s Hollywood bungalow ranch-style. We simply pulled up unannounced in his garden, bibbed the horn, and were waved indoors for a drink with the mayor and his family and friends. His tiny grandmother – well, someone's tiny grandmother – greeted me with peals of laughter, peals of laughter that erupted occasionally during our visit; she clearly found pale balding northerners an immense source of entertainment, and was still chuckling away when I left. Pano translated, and the (then) mayor, Basta, explained that there was already a court case in motion against the land-grabber, and that we would have to let the law take its course. Pano seemed satisfied with the answer, and I was happy to accept his satisfaction. I imagined the court case working its way through Greek law.

At Easter, the land-grabber began fencing the land off, and still nothing had been done by the courts. The court case against the land-grabber was burrowing slowly through the system towards its day in court, although if past experience was anything to go by even a finding against the businessman wouldn't deter him. Not one of the foreign owners was prepared to do anything physical; remove the fencing, open up the old path, rip up the illegal No Entry sign. (I still gave it a daily wallop.) Even Pano, who had become so angry at first, now counselled caution. Depressed, I began to wonder if I had got in too far over my head. Began to wonder if I should have got involved in the first place, touched a stone or shred of brush. I felt I was motivated by a sense of justice, but now began to wonder if it was any of my business at all. Somewhere in there lay the line that interlopers should not cross, and I wondered if I had strayed over it. It only heightened the sense of foolishness at committing myself to a place where I didn't and couldn't really belong. Briefly, and irrationally, I actually hated Paxos.

This was made all the more acute by the reasons why we visit Paxos. Writers from Doctor Johnson to Paul Fussell have theorised about the reasons we go on holiday to other places. Apart from the usual reasons people go on holiday, we have found Paxos to be an extraordinarily, perhaps even unreasonably, beautiful place to visit, and when it isn't embroiling us in land-grabs it could quite justifiably be described as a minor paradise. We have seen perhaps half the countries in the world between us, but have never come across anywhere so appealing as Paxos. All the factors – distance, accessibility, climate, landscape, culture, the cost of living, the attitude of the inhabitants towards tourists – make it an ideal place to go on holiday if you are prepared to forego nightlife, Safeway and modern plumbing. Indeed, the lack of these things is what keeps Paxos the way it is. Personally, we also find it a haven away from the new barbarism at large in Britain today, in its government and on its streets. This only makes returning from Paxos all the more depressing, however, and points up a further dislocation: what if we don't really belong at either end of the London-Paxos voyage?

All this questions our reasons for spending so much time on the island, even when it is legitimised by a project such as this book. We have more (and friendlier) neighbours on Paxos than we do in London, but does that make it 'home'? In his dedication to his film *Mediterraneo*, Gabriele Salvatore seemed to be making a virtue of the behaviour of 'all those who are running away', but that only seems to strengthen the power and inevitability of whatever it is they are running away from (the twentieth century). Are we 'coming home' to Lakka, or simply running away, fleeing the new level of Dante's Hell that London has become at the end of the millennium?

And imagining that we might find a means of housing and supporting ourselves in this culture and economy, could we really survive Paxos? Many have tried and failed, arriving with colour TVs and boxloads of books but still developing cabin fever before the winter was halfway through. Could I really go feral – I could never really become 'native' – and burn my bridges with Britain? Isn't my life too tied up with earning money working for magazines, trying to write, a life dressed by this Apple Mac computer, a large CD collection, art house cinemas, Compendium Books, the Institute of Contemporary Arts, Tower Records, the Camden Jazz Festival, Gay Pride, festivals of John Cage and early Peter Greenaway films, *Golden Girls* and *The Late Show*, Graham's irrational devotion to *Brookside* and mine to *Coronation Street*, the daily *Guardian*, spending sprees in Waterstone's, Marks and Spencer's latticed bacon and sausage flan? What of the dear friends we don't see enough of already?

The friends issue is a difficult one, short of having the room to invite them on a regular basis, and even then the nature of friendship is likely to change. I would like to think, however, that I might be able to improvise a cultural lifeline, although even that implies a failure in the nature of life on Paxos. It would be pleasant to think that life on Paxos might be about unloading all that cultural baggage, but that is naive. That culture, or at least the taste for it, is in our genes, and much of the intellectual life among the interlopers on Paxos is about establishing access to all that culture swirling around in the big cities of the north: be it a new novel, a k d lang album, videos of *Cheers*, even basic foodstuffs like plain brown flour or Marmite. These things are circulated and consumed by interlopers much in the way they are circulated and consumed by long-term hospital patients and guests of Her Majesty's prisons.

There is a further worry, a sort of *Invasion of the Bodysnatchers* infection that can be observed to affect many long-term interlopers. Would I end up as a wrinkled fascist in a sunhat? Distance, and perhaps a land-locked version of calenture, put funny ideas in people's heads. Despite there now being a generation of voters who have only ever known Conservative government, the consensus among the floral print and cavalry slacks brigade over their gin and tonics in the hills above Gaios is that the state of affairs in Britain today is akin to Daniel Ortega's Nicaragua at its revolutionary zenith.

Luckily, with relocation to Paxos still a dream fixed in an unspecified point in the future, these are usually just passing panic attacks, ruffling the calm of a May or September morning or afternoon in Lakka. They cast a doubt over the enterprise, but a problem acknowledged is a problem on the way to being solved, and we could only ever go feral here having surmounted those problems.

So we return to lotus eating, emptying the fridge on to the table for lunch, staring out at the endless ambient movie of Lakka bay, too Greeked out to do more than talk about the food. Sometimes, Graham and Don watch in amusement as my brain takes perhaps ten minutes to engage with the notion of eating. I just stare at the homemade bread and pickles, the meats and cheeses, the vegetables and fruits, the serried mayos and mustards, the boiled eggs and remnants of imported herrings, sausages, peanut butters, sandwich spreads, and, defeated, head for the bread and the last of the triangles of cream cheese.

This meal is an alternative heaven to the Scrabble game at sunset. Light from an explosion on a nearby star eight minutes ago fills the bay. The sailing school people are heading back for their siesta. The cicadas are revving up in the trees along the cliffs. The light waves in the blue spectrum wash sky and sea in a variety of light blues and whites. Corfu floats in the north. Castellated cumulus clouds climb 15, 20 miles into the sky over the mainland, threatening storms that will probably leave Paxos unharmed. Boats pass under the house. The cats and even the lizards are asleep, felled by the afternoon heat. Don pads off for his siesta, leaving us paralysed and blinded in the shade. Hours leak away. We could sit here for ever.